Africa
The Nile Route

by

Kim Naylor

Roger Lascelles, Cartographic and Travel Publisher
47 York Road, Brentford, Middlesex TW8 0QP Telephone: 01-847 0935

Publication Data

Title	Africa - The Nile Route
Typeface	Phototypeset in Compugraphic English 18
Photographs	By the author.
Printing	Kelso Graphics, Kelso, Scotland.
ISBN	09 903909 22 7
Edition	Nov. 1982, reprinted Nov. 1983
	and Aug 1986.
Publisher	Roger Lascelles
	47 York Road, Brentford, Middlesex, TW8 0QP.
Copyright	Kim Naylor

Distribution

Africa:	Enquiries invited	
Americas:	Canada —	International Travel Maps & Books, P.O. Box 2290, Vancouver B.C.
	U.S.A. —	Bradt Enterprises, 95 Harvey Street, Cambridge, MA. 02140
Asia:	Hong Kong —	The Book Society, G.P.O. Box 7804, Hong Kong Tel: 5-241901
	India —	English Book Store, New Delhi
Australasia	Australia —	Rex Publications, 413 Pacific Highway, Artarmon NSW 2064
	New Zealand —	International Travel Guides, P.O. Box 4397, Christchurch 1
Europe:	Belgium —	Brussels, Peuples et Continents
	GB/Ireland —	Available through all booksellers with a good foreign travel section.
	Italy —	Libreria dell'Automobile, Milano
	Netherlands —	Nilsson & Lamm BV, Weesp
	Denmark —	Copenhagen — Arnold Busck, G.E.C. Gad, Boghallen
	Finland —	Oslo - Arne Gimnes/J.G. Tanum
	Sweden —	Stockholm - Esselte/Akademi Bokhandel Fritzes/Hedengrens
		Gothenburg - Gumperts/Esselte
		Lund - Gleerupska
	Switzerland —	Basle Buchhandlung Bider
		Bern Atlas Reisebuchladen
		Geneva Librairie Artou
		Zurich The Travel Bookshop

Contents

Introduction

This guide book is directed at the 'low budget' traveller who is making the overland journey from Cairo, in Egypt, to Juba, in southern Sudan, and then on to Nairobi, the Kenyan capital. The main purpose of the guide is to provide information on visa formalities, health regulations, what to see, where to stay, where to eat and most important of all, how to get from A to B. In addition, there are brief sections on Sudan's history and tribes which give the visitor a starting point for further reading on the background of the country.

The section on Egypt deals with the trip up the Nile Valley from Cairo via Luxor to Aswan on the southern border. I have included a few pages on Alexandria because this city with its unique European and Arab mixture is an appropriate place to start — or finish — the journey.

To the south of Egypt is the vast Sudan, Africa's largest country. Under its present government, Sudan has recently caught the attention of the West. However, for the traveller, this fascinating part of Africa is little known. Most of the book deals with the Sudan: first, because there isn't a recent guide book to the country; and second travellers tend to regard Sudan merely as a stepping stone between Egypt and Kenya. It deserves more attention and I hope this book will encourage greater interest in the country.

The last few pages of the book cover the route from Sudan's south east border to Nairobi, and a short summary of Kenya's two main attractions: the game parks and the coast.

Although the account of the route has been written from north to south, there is no reason why the journey should be made in reverse, from Nairobi to Cairo.

MEDITERRANEAN SEA

THE ROUTE
FROM CAIRO
TO NAIROBI

CAIRO

EGYPT

ASWAN

LAKE
ASWAN

WADI
HALFA

RED SEA

NILE

KHARTOUM

BLUE NILE

SUDAN

WHITE NILE

JUBA

N

UGANDA

LAKE
TURKANA

KENYA

LAKE
VICTORIA

NAIROBI

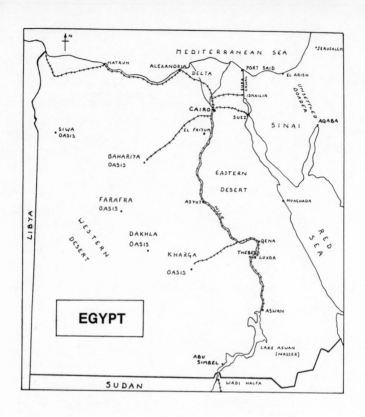

Part 1
Egypt

Contents: Egypt

Egypt — Basic Information

Area: 998,000 sq. km. (Gt. Britain is 230,609 sq. km)

Population: 41 million (1980): Cairo nine million, Alexandria two and a half million, Aswan 150,000. Ninety-nine per cent of the population lives in the Nile Valley, Delta and oases regions (a total of only 35,000 sq. km). Over half the population is under fourteen years old.

Geography: Egypt is divided into four main geographical regions: the Valley (Upper Egypt) and Delta (Lower Egypt) of the Nile: the Libyan or Western Desert; the Arabian or Eastern Desert, and the Sinai Peninsula. Egypt also owns several islands in the Gulf of Suez.

Language: Arabic is the official language, although English and French are widely spoken.

Religion: Ninety per cent of Egyptians are Muslim (mainly Sunni); the majority of the remaining ten per cent is Coptic Christian.

Government: Egypt is a Democratic Socialist State with a 360 member Assembly.

Head of State is President Hosni Mubarak.

Economy: The economy is based on agriculture, with nearly sixty per cent of the population dependent on the land. Agriculture (mainly cotton) accounts for fifty per cent of the country's exports.

Income (per capita): $310 (1976)

Time: GMT + 2 hours

Electricity: 220 volts A.C.

1. The Country

Today — as throughout history — the Egyptian civilization owes its existence to the regular flow of the Nile.

The Nile dramatically dissects the country's deserts from south to north. Over ninety-eight per cent of Egypt's population live and work on the river's narrow fertile flood plains.

For the tourist, the pyramids, tombs, temples, churches and mosques clustered on the Nile's banks reveal the magnificence of Egypt's long and fascinating history.

Climate

From November to March, Egypt's average temperature during the day is 17°C. It's cold at night, so it's advisable to take warm clothing. From April to October the average temperature during the day is 32°C.

Cairo and Upper Egypt have a hot. dry climate (in the summer temperatures can exceed 40°C) with little rain (less than 25 mm) and a low humidity. Alexandria and the northern coast have a Mediterranean climate with some heavy rains in winter.

The unpleasant **Khamasin** (the strong wind that carries dust storms) is common during April and May.

The best time to visit Egypt is between October and April.

Temperatures

	January		August	
	min.	max.	min.	max.
Alexandria	9°C	18°C	23°C	30°C
Cairo	9°C	19°C	22°C	35°C
Aswan	8°C	24°C	25°C	42°C

History

In the predynastic era Egypt was divided into the two kingdoms of Upper Egypt and Lower Egypt. The dynastic period began with the unification of the kingdoms. Dates given below for the Old and Middle Kingdoms are very approximate.

Old Kingdom

3200 BC	1st dynasty (from This)	Age of Menes and the founding of Memphis
3000 BC	2nd dynasty (from This)	
2800 BC	3rd dynasty (from Memphis)	Zoser builds the Step Pyramid at Sakkara
2700 BC	4th dynasty (from Memphis)	Age of the Great Pyramids of Giza (Cheops, Chepren and Mycernius)
2575 BC	5th dynasty (from Elephantine)	Prominence of sun worship
2400 BC	6th dynasty (from Memphis)	
2200 BC	First Intermediate Period	7th and 8th dynasties from Memphis, 9th and 10th dynasties from Heracleopolis in Upper Egypt

Middle Kingdom

2100 BC	11th dynasty (from Thebes)	The Theban king defeats the king of Heracleopolis
2000 BC	12th dynasty (from Thebes)	A prosperous period in Egypt. The southern border is established at the Second Cataract; Sesostris III builds forts between the First and Second Cataracts. The prominence of the God, Amun.
1800 BC	Second Intermediate Period	13th to 17th dynasty. The Hyksos, Asiatic settlers, rise up and rule the Delta region from the 14th to 17th dynasty

New Kingdom

1600 BC	18th dynasty (from Thebes)	Hyksos expelled from Egypt. The building of lavish temples to the God Amun.
c.1515 BC		Thutmose I is the first king to build his tomb at the Valley of the Kings
		Amenophis III builds the Temple of Saddenga in Sudan
1352-1344 BC		Tutankhamun reigns
1305 BC	19th dynasty (from Thebes)	Rameses II builds the rock-hewn temple at Abu Simbel
1200 BC	20th dynasty (from Thebes)	Towards the end of the dynasty Egypt is divided between the High Priest of Amun at Thebes and the nominal king, Smendes, at Tanis in the Delta

Late Dynastic Period

1085 BC	21st dynasty (from Thebes and Tanis)	
945 BC	22nd dynasty (from Bubastis)	Sheshonq I, of Libyan origin, gains control over the priests at Thebes The 22nd, 23rd, 24th, and 25th dynasties to some extent overlapped
745 BC	23rd dynasty (from Tanis)	Priests of Amun flee from Thebes to Napata (Sudan) and persuade King Plankhi to invade the unsettled Egypt
718 BC	24th dynasty (from Sais in the Delta)	
712 BC	25th dynasty (from Napata and later from Thebes)	Piankhi conquers Egypt
665 BC	26th dynasty (from Sais)	An Assyrian invasion eventually leads to Psammetichus becoming the first king of the dynasty. This is known as the Saite Period — an era of

		revived splendour for Egypt
525 BC	27th dynasty (from Persia)	Cambyses of Persia conquers Egypt
404 BC	28th dynasty (from Sais)	Only one king reigns during this dynasty — Amyrtaeus, who expels the Persians
399 BC	29th and 30th dynasties (from Mendes and Sebennytus respectively, in the Delta region)	The kings of this period enlist the help of the Greeks to keep out the Persians in the Delta
343 BC	Persian rule	Persians reconquer Egypt; their rule is ended by Alexander the Great in 332 BC

Ptolemies

323 BC	Ptolemy Soter, Alexander's general, becomes Satrap of Egypt on the death of Alexander
48 BC	Julius Caesar first enters Egypt
44 BC	Death of Caesar
30 BC	Death of Mark Antony and Cleopatra, who was the last of the Ptolemies

Roman and Byzantine Periods

30 BC	
AD 61	St. Mark preaches Christianity in Egypt for the first time. For the next three hundred years Christians suffer intermittent persecution
AD 378	Theodosius I proclaims Christianity the religion of his Empire
AD 400	Christianity linked with Constantinople
AD 451	The Council of Chalcedon: the Copts remain Monophysites

| AD 480 | Persians invade Egypt |
| AD 622 | Mohammed's flight from Mecca to Medina |

Mohammedan Period

AD 640		Amr ibn al Asi, the Arab, conquers Egypt
AD 661	Omayyad Khalifahs	
AD 750	Abbasid Khalifahs	
AD 868	Tulunid Khalifahs	
AD 905	Ikhshidids	
AD 969	Fatamid Khalifahs	
AD 1171	Ayyubid Khalifahs	Saladin, founder of this dynasty, fortifies Cairo and builds the Citadel. He reigns twenty-three years, but spends only eight in Egypt.
AD 1250	Bahrite Mamluks	Mamluks were originally slaves either bought or captured in war
AD 1382	Circassian Mamluks	

Turkish Rule (1517-1879)

AD 1547	The Turks occupy Cairo
AD 1798-1801	Brief French occupation
AD 1798	Napoleon's victory at the Battle of the Pyramids
AD 1805	Mohammed Ali becomes ruler of Egypt (nominally the country is still part of the Ottoman Empire) and establishes a family dynasty which lasts until 1952
AD 1869	The Suez Canal is completed during the reign of Khedive Ismail

British Occupation

1882	British and French rivalry for Egypt leads to Egypt becoming a British protectorate
1922	Egypt given a Constitutional monarchy
	Anti-British feeling grows after Second World War
1952	King Farouk forced to abdicate

The Republic

1952	After the Neguib-Nasser coup d'état complete independence is gained and Mohammed Neguib becomes head of state
1953	Egypt declared a Republic
1954	Neguib deposed. Gamal Nasser becomes President
1970	Nasser dies. Anwar Sadat becomes President
1981	Sadat assassinated in Cairo

Muntazah Palace, Alexandria: This was a royal palace up until King Farouk's abdication in 1952. It is now a presidential residence.

2. Information for Travellers

Visas and registration

Visas are essential for entry into Egypt and are issued within twenty-four hours; two passport photographs are required. In London a visa costs £5 sterling and is available from the Consulate of the Arab Republic of Egypt, 19 Kensington Palace Gardens, London W8; tel: 01 229 8818.

When you apply for a visa you are asked how long you want to stay in Egypt and the visa is issued for the period you state (up to a maximum of thirty days).

If you are flying direct to Cairo, visas are obtainable on entry. However, there are two problems: first you may be asked to change $US150 (or the equivalent) into Egyptian pounds at the airport bank; second, the immigration officer may not grant you a full one-month visa.

Although the visa is usually valid for a month, you are entitled to an additional two-week grace period before having to leave the country.

Visa extensions

Extensions are available for a few piastres from the Mugamma Building in Tahrir Square, Cairo, and passport offices in main provincial towns. You are asked for bank receipts to prove that you have exchanged $US150 (or the equivalent) into Egyptian currency. Without this evidence the extension won't be granted.

A Transit Visa lasts seven days and costs £E2. You are not required to change money.

Registration

You have to register within a week of entering Egypt. The triangle of acceptance is stamped in your passport at the Mugamma Building in Tahrir Square, Cairo (most hotels will send somebody to get this for you). Without it you are liable to a £E5 fine on departure.

If you are coming from Israel and going to Sudan, see p. 104 in the Sudan Section.

Money

The Egyptian pound (£E) is divided into 100 piastres (PT). Money is circulated in the following denominations:

> notes: 1, 5, 10, 20, 50, 100 Egyptian pounds;
> notes: 5, 10, 25, 50 piastres
> coins: ½, 1, 2, 5, 10, 20, 25, 50 piastres.

The exchange rate is £E1.50 per pound sterling, 75PT per US dollar. You may bring as much foreign currency into the country as you like and up to £E20 in cash. Money and valuables must be declared on Form D on arrival. You may be asked to submit the form on departure, although this is particularly unlikely if you are going overland into Sudan. Egyptian pounds may be reconverted into a foreign currency when you leave the country, but at a poor rate. However, it's illegal to be in possession of Egyptian pounds on departure.

Banking hours are 9 am to 12.30 pm, Monday to Thursday and Saturday; 10 am to 12 noon Sunday; closed Friday. Banks throughout the country exchange travellers cheques.

A number of Western banks (American Express, Barclays, and Credit Suisse, for example) have branches in Cairo. It is simpler to have money sent out to you via an international bank than the post office.

Throughout the country you will be pestered by (illegal) street dealers who offer a twenty per cent higher rate for hard currency than the banks. If you decide to deal with them, make sure you are not short changed.

Costs

Egypt is a very cheap country in which to travel. If you are prepared to do without luxuries, then £E3 to £E4 is adequate for a cheap central hotel in Cairo and three basic meals a day. The visitor who wants the comforts of a three star hotel, three course meals at a mid-price restaurant and first or second class train transport (with airconditioning) will still find Egypt far cheaper than Europe.

Students with International Students Card are eligible for a fifty percent reduction in rail fares and fifty percent off entrance fees to most museums and sites.

Post Offices

Post offices are open from 8.30 to 3 pm, daily; closed Friday. An aerogramme costs 14PT; allow a week for it to reach Europe. A poste restante service is provided at post offices throughout the country. In Cairo, this is at the main post office in Ataba Square; a more reliable alternative is American Express, 15 Kasr El Nil. Red letter boxes are for letters within Egypt; green boxes are for express mail, blue for air mail.

International phone calls can be made from the phone booths in Alfy Street.

There is a telegram office opposite the post office in Ataba Square.

Embassies

British: 2 Ahmed Raghed Street, Garden City; tel: 28850
Australian: 1097 Corniche El Nil Street, Garden City; tel: 22862
American: 5 Latin America Street, Garden City; tel: 28219
Kenyan: 8 Madina Al Monawara Street, Dokki; tel: 859546
Sudanese: 1 Mohamed Fahmi Street, Garden City; tel: 25043

Egyptian holidays

The Muslim lunar calendar has only 354 or 355 days — consequently Muslim holidays (marked by an asterisk) fall ten to twelve days earlier every year on the Gregorian calendar. The holiday dates are for 1982. Muslim holidays are approximate.

*Moulid El Nabi (the Prophet's birthday)	8th January
Union Day	22nd February
Shem El Nassim (spring festival)	mid April (1 day)
Labour Day	1st May
Evacuation Day	18th June
*Eids El Fitr	21st-24th July
Revolution Anniversary	23rd July
Libyan Revolution Day	1st September
*Eid El Adha (Korban Bairam)	29th September - 2nd October
Armed Forces Day	6th October
*Islamic New Year	18th October
Suez Day	24th October
Victory Day	23rd December

El Dahan Restaurant, Khan El Khalili, Cairo: Many of Cairo's traditional restaurants are frequented by foreigners. Dishes such as kebabs and kofta are popular and are generally good and cheap.

Opening Hours

Government offices are open from 9 am to 2 pm; daily except Fridays; banks from 9 am to 12.30 pm, Monday to Thursday and Saturday and 10 am to 12 noon, Sunday. Many shops are open on Friday; shops' opening hours are from 9 am to 1 pm and 5 pm to 8.30 pm.

Health

Vaccinations against cholera and yellow fever are required before arrival in Egypt only for people travelling from an infected area.

Vaccinations are available from the health unit at the Continental Hotel in Opera Square, Cairo for persons travelling to infected areas.

There are a few precautions that should be taken:

Do not swim in the Nile: bilharzia is one of several diseases prevalent in the river. Treat all cuts immediately. Avoid fresh salads at less reputable restaurants and food stalls as these often cause stomach upsets.

Food

Baklawa comprises layers of pastry with almonds and walnuts.
Cossa is courgettes stuffed with chopped mutton.
Dolma are vine leaves stuffed with meat.
Felafel (taemiya) are burgers made from ground **ful** beans and fried.
Ful (field beans) is a stable food in Egypt and is usually boiled and served with oil and lemon.
Kebabs are grilled lamb or mutton.
Kosheri is rice with lentils and sometimes spaghetti and meat.
Mahallbiya is a popular cold rice pudding.
Tahina is sesame houmus.

Drink

Chai is tea.
Kawa is Coffee, usually served Turkish style. **Ziada** means sweet; **masbuth** is 'just right'; **saada** is without sugar.
The juice bars are one of the greatest luxuries in Egypt. A glass of pure, fresh juice (orange, grapefruit, guava), costs 15PT.

Tap water is chlorinated and therefore safe to drink.

Alcohol is readily available in Egypt. A litre bottle of the Egyptian Stella beer costs 85PT.

Entering Egypt

By sea to Alexandria

Alexandria Navigation (35 Piccadilly, London W1; tel: 01 734-4619. Also George A. Callitsis, Piraeus; and 2 El Nasr Street, Alexandria.) has two sailings a month from Naples and Venice via Piraeus. You can sail A, B, or C tourist classes or deck class. Deck-class fare (summer only) from Naples is £80, Venice £68 and Piraeus £40 (all include meals). Tourist-class fares range from £55 to £140.

Adriatic Line has three or four sailings a month from Venice via Piraeus. The youth fare for people under twenty-six (cabin) is £118 from Venice, £65 from Piraeus.

Adriatic Line agents are Sealink Holidays, Victoria Station, London SW1; tel: 01 828 1948; Gilnavi Agency Ltd, 97 Akti Miaouli and Favierou, Piraeus, Athens; Sayed de Castro Company Shipping, 33 Salah Salem Street, Alexandria.

By air to Cairo

Flights leave Athens daily for Cairo. Many airlines — for instance, Olympic, Egyptian, TWA, Ethiopian — offer a youth fare for people under twenty-six for £30 sterling. Scheduled flights from London start from £120 (£195 return) on Malev, the Hungarian airline. **Leaving Cairo:** If you buy an international air ticket in Egypt you must have bank receipts to prove that you have converted the fare from hard currency into Egyptian pounds. There is a £E3 airport departure tax.

Cairo airport is situated 22 km north east of the city centre. Allow thirty minutes to reach the airport from the centre of Cairo (at least an hour during the rush-hour). Buses 400 (from opposite the museum in Tahrir Square) and 410 from Opera Square leave every thirty minutes (every hour at night) for the airport. The journey by limousine (Limousine Misr, tel: 835174) costs £E5.

You are allowed to sleep in the main hall of the airport — an advantage if you have an early-morning flight. The airport banks, post office and cafe are open twenty-four hours.

Overland from Israel

Tel Aviv to Al Arish is three hours by bus and costs 40 shekels. There are a few hundred metres of no man's land between Israel and Egypt at Al Arish across which you are obliged to take a bus (4 shekels). You may have to change $US150 (or the equivalent) into Egyptian currency at the border.

A shared taxi from Al Arish to Cairo costs £E5 and takes about six hours depending how long it takes you to cross the Suez Canal. You can break your journey to Cairo at El Quantara on the Suez Canal and resume it from the other side of the canal .

In the present international situation, the circumstances of travel between Israel and Egypt are liable to change.

By ferry from Sudan
The ferry from Wadi Halfa, Sudan, arrives at Aswan harbour. From here trains depart for Aswan town and on to Luxor and Cairo.

Transport Around the Country

Trains
Rail transport in Egypt is very cheap, reasonably punctual and of a standard — in the sleepers and in first and air conditioned second class — comparable to trains in Europe. Third class carriages have wooden seats and are extremely crowded.

For first and second class seats reserve your ticket at least a day before departure; book several days in advance for a sleeper compartment. There are no third class reservations.

To give some idea of train prices, here are some fares from Cairo:

			Sleeper	
Journey	1st class	2nd class	1st class	2nd class
Alexandria (208 km)	£E3.00	£E1.75		
Luxor (680 km)	£E8.20	£E4.40	£E17.65	£E10.30
Aswan (900 km)	£E10.50	£E6.00	£E17.65	£E10.30

The fares above are for air-conditioned compartments.

Second class (without air-conditioning) and third class fares are approximately two thirds and one third respectively of the second class 'air conditioned' fare.

A new tourist train is now in operation.

If you have a through ticket, you are allowed to break your journey at an intermediate station. Before resuming your trip, have your ticket endorsed at the booking office.

Students are eligible for a fifty per cent reduction in rail fares upon presentation of an International Student Card — or equivalent — at the ticket office.

Nearly all stations have left luggage facilities.

Buses
Buses of various standards operate throughout the country.

Collective taxis
Collective taxis usually depart from near the railway station or bus terminal. The driver waits until he has five people going to the same destination before leaving. The fare is much the same as that for a second-class ticket in an air-conditioned compartment.

Internal Flights
Egyptair operates reasonably priced daily flights to Luxor (£E56.40), Aswan (£E79.20), Abu Simbel (£E112.20) and Hurghada (£E61.30). These prices are as at February 1982 and are for the round trip.

Nile Steamers
At present only luxury steamers (operated by organizations such as the Nile Hilton) make the journey into Upper Egypt. These cruises are very expensive and usually oversubscribed. A very pleasant trip is by **felucca** between Luxor and Aswan (see p. 69).

3. Cairo

Cairo, at the apex of the Nile Delta, is Egypt's capital and Africa's largest city, with a population of 9 million.

What is most striking about Cairo — apart from the crowds, noise and general bustle — is that, first, it is cosmopolitan. There's truth in the cliche, 'Cairo is the meeting point of Africa and Arabia, Europe and Asia'. The second striking feature is the clear evidence of the different periods of history in the environs of the city: from the Pharaonic pyramids at Giza through to the European-influenced centre of the city.

Getting around

Most places of interest in central Cairo are within walking distance of the downtown area (around Midan Tahrir and Midan Talaat Harb): Rameses Square (railway station) is a twenty-minute walk, Khan El Khalili and Islamic Cairo also twenty minutes, Garden City ten minutes' walk. Buses are very crowded; taxis are quite cheap, but before embarking on your journey check the correct fare with a local.

Where to stay

Despite Cairo's many small, cheap hotels, it can be difficult (especially in winter) to find somewhere to stay. For this reason a list of low-priced, centrally located hotels is given below. Most of them have between fifteen and thirty rooms and offer basic and adequate accommodation.

The following are hotels where you can expect to pay from £E2 to £E4 per night for a single room.

The **Ashbilia** (16 Adly Street; tel: 916942) does not have single rooms but dormitories, each containing four to six beds. A small, clean establishment.

The **Beausite** (27 Talaat Harb Street — almost opposite the National Hotel; tel: 749916) has a shower for every two rooms. It's clean and good value for money.

For visitors to Cairo aged between twenty and thrity, the **Golden** (13 Talaat Harb Street — opposite the Wimpy bar; tel: 742659) is a well known landmark. Its reputation is due to the hospitality and helpfulness of its octogenarian owner, Mr. Fares. Single and double rooms have private bathrooms; there are also dormitories.

After the Golden, the **Oxford** (32 Talaat Harb Street — near the Zeina café; tel: 53173) is the best known of the cheap hotels and charges £E2.25 for a double room, £E1.25 for a bed in a dormitory.

The **Roma** (169 Mohammed Farid Street — 50 m before the junction of 26th July Street) has large, quiet rooms and a somewhat sombre atmosphere.

Abu Simbel is a ten-storey hotel in Ataba Square. Few foreigners stay there — the rooms aren't all that clean; there are invariably vacancies.

Other inexpensive hotels include: the **Minerva** (39 Talaat Harb Street — down the alley just before 26th July Street; tel: 7451234); the **Plaza** (37 Kasr El Nil Street); the **Select** (19 Adly Street); **Ismailia House** (on the east side of Tahrir Square, in the same building as the Astra Café, on the eighth floor; tel: 27988).

There is also a **Youth Hostel** in Abdel Aziz al Saud Street, El Manial (on the Northern part of Roda Island, at the foot of El Gamaa Bridge — 2¼ km south east of Tahrir Square). A bed in a dormitory costs 85PT.

The following are hotels where you can expect to pay from £E4 to £E6 for a single room.

Lunapark (65 Gumhuriya Street — between Rameses Square and Opera Square; tel: 918628) is a small, good value, modern hotel.

The **Anglo Suisse** (14 Champollion Street; tel: 751497); **Des Roses** (33 Talaat Harb Street; tel: 978922); **Garden City House** (23 Kamaledin Salah, Garden City; tel: 281126); **Suisse** (26 Mohammed Bassouni Street; tel: 743153); **Tulip** (3 Talaat Harb Square; tel: 758504); **Viennoise** (11 Mohammed Bassouni Street; tel: 743153).

Cairo has many middle range hotels, such as the Windsor in Alfy Street (£E10 for a single room), and quite a few first class hotels: the Meridien, part of the international chain of French hotels, the well known, nostalgic Shepheards and the Nile Hilton, all of which are on Corniche El Nil Street. Expect to pay £E50 per night for a single night at any of these hotels.

A list of middle-range and expensive hotels is available from the Tourist Office, 5 Adly Street.

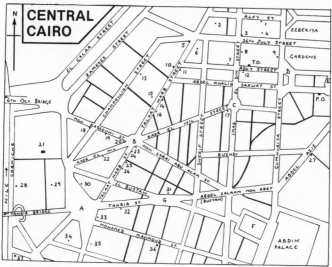

Main Squares

A Tahrir Square
B Talaat Harb Square
C Mustafa Kamel Square
D Opera Square
E Ataba Square
F Gumhuriya Square
G Falaki Square

Restaurants and Cafes

2 El Chimi
3 L'Americaine Cafe
4 Ali Hassan Al Hati
5 L'Americaine Cafe
15 Fu Shing
16 Indian Tea Centre
20 Groppi
24 Riches Bar
25 Felefela
27 Hag Mohamoud El Sammak
31 Domiati
32 Faterine El Tahrir

Hotels

6 Minerva
7 Select
8 Roma
9 Continental
10 Oxford Pension
11 Des Roses
12 Ashbilia
14 Beausite
17 Plaza
18 Anglo Suisse
19 Viennoise
23 Tulip
26 Golden
28 Nile Hilton
33 Ismailia House
37 Shepheards

Other Important Locations

1 Public Telephones
13 Egyptian Youth Centre
21 Egyptian Museum
22 American Express
29 Bus Terminals
30 Ticket Office for Buses to Alexandria
34 Mogamma Buildings
35 American University
36 Bab El Luk Station

T.O. Tourist Office
P.O. Post Office

Talaat Harb Street, Cairo: In stark contrast to Islamic Cairo, Talaat Harb Street is in the centre of Cairo's Westernized downtown. Heavy traffic and crowded pavements are characteristic of Cairo.

30

Where to eat

Ful, felafel, macaroni, basic meat dishes and **kosheri** can be eaten at the many cafeterias and pavement stalls: 20PT pays for a filling meal. Some cafeterias in the city centre at Excelsior, Bamboo, Zeina, Zed — all in Talaat Harb Street. The restaurants mentioned below are central, popular and moderately priced.

The following specialise in **ful** and **felafel** dishes: Al Domiata (Badrawi Building, Midan El Falaki) is popular with Cairenes. Felafela (15 Hoda Shaaraway Street — off Talaat Harb Street) serves an extensive Egyptian menu; it has a pleasant decor and caters largely for tourists. El Tabia (31 Orabi Street) enjoys a good reputation amongst Cairenes.

The following specialise in **kebab** and **kofta** dishes: Abou Shakra (69 Kasr El Aina Street) is closed during Ramadan. Ali Hassan Al Hati (8 Halim Street — behind Cicurel department store) is recommended partly because of the elegant decor — long chandeliers and mirrored walls. El Chimi (45 Midan Orabi) and El Dahan (4 Khan El Khalili) also serve good food.

Other value-for-money restaurants include: Faterine El Tahrir (166 Tahrir Street) serves Egyptian pancakes (**fater**), pastries stuffed with cheese, eggs, honey or an assortment of other fillings. Hag Mohamoud El Sammak (Abdel Aziz Street — opposite Omar Effendi) is a recommended seafood restaurant. Fu Shing (off Talaat Harb Street) is a cheap, popular Chinese restaurant.

Increasing numbers of restaurants are serving European dishes; most of the better ones are to be found in the top hotels. Kentucky Fried Chicken and Wimpy have sprung up in the last few years.

El Muizzlidin: Locals set up their market stalls amongst some of Egypt's most historic mosques and buildings.
The Cairene often takes these surroundings for granted whilst the tourist contemplates such links with the past in fascination.

Tea Houses

These serve tea, coffee (**espresso, capuccino, café au lait**) and often continental breakfast. Most have patisseries.

The following are popular Cairo tea houses.

L'Americaine (corner of 26th July Street and Talaat Harb Street, and corner of 26th July Street and Mohamed Farid Street);

Brazilian Coffee Shop (38 Talaat Harb Street and 12 26th July Street);

Groppi (Midan Talaat Harb Street) is the most famous and elegant teahouse in Cairo;

Indian Tea House (23 Talaat Harb Street) serves Indian tea and snacks;

Lappas (17 Kasr El Nil Street).

Traditional Egyptian cafés serving Turkish coffee and offering **shishas** (water pipes) are found throughout the city. The most famous is Fishawi's in Khan El Khalili near El Hussein Mosque.

Bars

There are many bars downtown. These usually shut at 11 p.m. Riches, Talaat Harb Street, is very popular.

Shopping

Sharia Muski starts at Ataba Square and continues into the heart of Islamic Cairo. It is along this road, dating from the days when Saladin encouraged foreign merchants to trade in the city, that Cairo's famous oriental bazaars are situated. **Khan El Khalili,** just east of Sayed El Hussein Mosque, is the best known and most interesting section (especially for handicrafts). The Muski, with its narrow alleys, is divided into areas, each one specialising in particular goods — gold, silver, copper, spices, perfumes, etc. Cotton, gold, leather goods, perfumes and saffron are the best value and most popular buys in Egypt. Prices are generally lower and merchandise of a better quality than similar articles in Sudan.

For a no-nonsense deal when buying Pharaonic souvenirs and Egyptian objet d'art, Onnig Alixanian's (in the courtyard of the Egyptian Musuem) fixed prices are surprisingly good value.

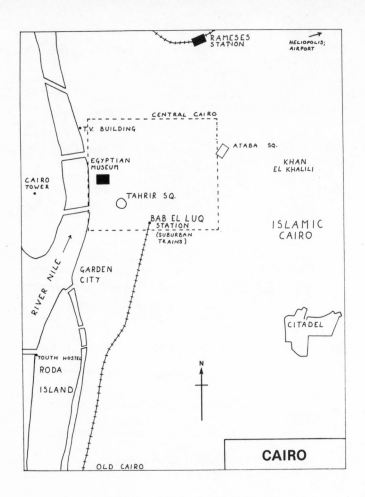

RAMESES STATION

HELIOPOLIS; AIRPORT

CENTRAL CAIRO

T.V. BUILDING

EGYPTIAN MUSEUM

CAIRO TOWER

ATABA SQ.

KHAN EL KHALILI

TAHRIR SQ.

BAB EL LUQ STATION (SUBURBAN TRAINS)

ISLAMIC CAIRO

RIVER NILE

GARDEN CITY

YOUTH HOSTEL

RODA ISLAND

CITADEL

N

OLD CAIRO

CAIRO

Most of the perfume shops do not supply natural essences — whatever their owners may say. The unpretentious Kassabians (halfway along Sharia Klut Bey) sell essences of popular scents such as Rive Gauche and the Chanel range as well as the usual heavy Arabian perfumes.

Cotton can be bought and tailored at many shops. Ouf (in Khan El Khalili by the first walkway over El Azhar) has a good reputation for off-the-peg garments at a reasonable price.

Night Clubs

The top belly dancers perform at the expensive clubs (for instance the **Nile Hilton** and **Sheraton** hotels). For an equally entertaining evening — largely due to the atmosphere of the audience — there are cheaper clubs in 26th July Street (**Palmyra,** for example).

Discos

Most of the best discos are in the top hotels. **After Eight** (6 Kasr El Nil Street) has a good reputation.

Where to go for more information

The Tourist Office is at 5 Adly Street; tel: 923 000.

Information on films (several cinemas show recent English films), exhibitions, lectures (such as those in the Cultural Centres) can be found in the daily **Egyptian Gazette.**

Pharaonic Cairo

On the west bank of the Nile from Abu Rawash (15 km east of Cairo to El Lisht 40 km to its south) is a raised tract of land on the edge of the Libyan Desert. It is along here that the pyramids of Abu Rawash, Giza, Zawat El Aryan, Abusir, Sakkara, Dahshur and Lisht were built. This is where most of Egypt's pyramids are to be found.

The Egyptian Museum houses the world's largest collection of Pharaonic art. It is a pity that the overwhelming number of exhibits — which include the magnificent Golden Mask of Tutankhamon — are displayed with such nonchalance. The museum is situated in the centre of Cairo near the Hilton Hotel in Tahrir Square, and is open from 9 am to 4 pm daily: closed 11 am to 1 pm, Friday. Entrance: £E2. A wide range of printed guides to the museum is available at the entrance to the museum.

Situated at Giza on the edge of Cairo, 16 km SW of the city centre, the **Pyramids of Giza** (built — as were all pyramids — as tombs) are the most famous and regarded as one of the Seven Wonders of the Ancient World. Napoleon estimated that the stone from the three pyramids could build a 3 m wall around the perimeter of France.

At the Pyramids the unsuspecting tourist is swamped by so-called antique and souvenir dealers, guides, and horsemen or camelmen offering rides on their animals. Initially they all ask grossly exaggerated prices for their wares or services. Find out from a local what a fair deal is and then — like everywhere else in Egypt — be prepared to bargain.

The **Great (Cheops) Pyramid** was built by Pharoah Cheops as his own tomb in 2690 BC. It is 137 m high and covers an area of 13 acres. Without any form of cement or mortar, it took 100,000 men twenty years to construct this massive monument. Some of the two-and-a-half million stone blocks weigh as much as 30 tons each.

The **Chepren Pyramid** still retains the granite casing on its peak which originally covered the entire structure. It was built by King Chepren in 2650 BC and stands 136 m.

The **Mycerinus Pyramid** was built by King Mycerinus in 2600 BC; at 65 m it is the smallest of the three pyramids.

The pyramids can be entered from the north side. They are open from 8 am to 5 pm. Entrance to the Great Pyramid: £E2.

Situated 350 m south east of the Great Pyramid, the **Sphinx** was carved from natural rock and is in the shape of a recumbent lion — symbolizing majesty — with a man's head — symbolizing intelligence. The Sphinx stands 20 m high and is 57 m long. It was built by King Chepren in honour of the Sun god, Horus, and faces east to catch the first rays of sunrise. Most of the facial damage was caused by the Mamelukes during their shooting practice. Between the legs of the Sphinx is the 'Dream Stele' of King Tuthmosis IV. The stele tells of how the king was resting on a pile of sand when a god appeared to him in a vision. The God told him that if he cleared the sand he would reveal the Sphinx and later become King of Egypt — a prophecy which was fulfilled.

The **Son et Lumiere** takes place daily (except Friday) at 7.30 p.m. It is a well delivered historical commentary on the Pyramids and the Sphinx, along with a dramatic lighting display of the monuments. Programmes in English are on Monday, Wednesday and Saturday; in French on Monday (8.30 p.m.) and Tuesday, and in German on Sunday and Thursday. (This timetable is subject to change). Entrance: £E2. The show lasts one hour.

A return bus especially for the Son et Lumiere show leaves Tahrir Square (outside the Hilton Hotel); check at the Hilton for time of departure. Bus no.900 from Tahrir Square (opposite the Mogamma Building) also goes to the Pyramids.

The ruins of the ancient capital of **Memphis** lie 22 km south of Cairo. The city, dating from about 3200 BC, was built at the apex of the Delta. The soils were fertile: Pliny talked of trees so large that three men with extended arms couldn't encircle them. Most important of all was that Memphis, on the western bank, had the Nile as a natural defence from attacks from Syria and Arabia in the east. Even so the city was invaded on many occasions — the Napatan king, Piankhi, from Sudan was one such conqueror. It's not until the New Kingdom that Thebes takes over as the main centre.

Sakkara was the necropolis of Memphis. It's named after Saker, an ancient Egyptian god of death. The site, one of the most historic in Egypt, consists of fourteen pyramids and numerous tombs and mastabas from between the 1st and 30th dynasties (the 3rd and 4th dynasties were the golden periods for Memphis). It was here in 1976 that the oldest mummy (four thousand years old) was discovered.

The Step Pyramid was built in the 3rd dynasty as a tomb for King Zoser. The six-stepped 64m pyramid predates the pyramids of Giza and is the most important monument of its age.

El Muizzlidin, Cairo: The centuries old bustling markets in and around El Muizzlidin, Islamic Cairo, provide a fascinating example of the traditional Cairene way of life.

The Unas Pyramid is south east of the Step pyramid. Unas was the last king of the 5th dynasty. The walls of the burial chamber are covered with hieroglyphic inscriptions, known as the pyramid texts.

The Teta Pyramid is located north east of the Step pyramid and is the tomb of the first king of the 4th dynasty. It was built near the ruins of the prison where the Patriarch Joseph was detained.

The Serapeum Pyramid dating back to the 26th dynasty, contains vaults 3 m wide and nearly 6 m high where the Apis bulls from Memphis were buried. Twenty-four sarcophagi (4 m by 2 m by 3 m) remain on either side of the chambers.

The Tomb of Ti is situated north east of the Serapheum. Ti was a distinguished royal councillor in the 5th dynasty. The beautiful wall reliefs in his tomb depict everyday life in ancient Egypt.

The Tomb of Ptahotep is near Mariette's house. Ptahatep was a priest in the 6th dynasty. The wall reliefs show him carrying out his daily duties.

The Tomb of Mereruka, north east of the Step pyramid, is that of a high court official (5th dynasty). The wall paintings represent hunting and cattle herding.

Sakkara is situated 25 km south of Cairo. The easiest and cheapest way of getting there from the centre of town is by bus no. 124 from outside the Mugamma Building in Tahrir Square to Giza railway station. From here take a country taxi to El Badrashein (Memphis); then it's another cab ride (or a 4km. walk) directly east to Sakkara. There is a train service from Rameses Station to El Badrashein.

A desert track runs from the Pyramids of Giza, 16 km south to Sakkara. Horses and camels can be hired from opposite the Mena House Hotel by the Pyramids. Check with the tourist office, tour agents or other tourists how much to pay the guide for the 3½-hour journey. On the way you pass the derelict pyramid of Zawiyet El Aryan, the 5th dynasty sun sanctury at Abu Gurab, and the pyramids of Abusir. The pyramids of Dahshur lie 10km south of Sakkara.

The cobbled alleys of Old Cairo — the traditional Christian (Coptic) area of the city — have changed little over the centuries. The holy Family is reputed to have stayed here when they fled to Egypt.

Old Cairo

The Christian, or Coptic, colony of Old Cairo is located within the walls of the fortress of Babylon on the east bank, 3½ km south of the city centre. In the last centuries BC, the fortress of Babylon stood on the hill just south of Cairo. The waters of the Nile slowly receded and by the first century AD supplying water to the fortress became impractical. A small town with a Jewish community, known as Zoan, grew up below the fort on the east bank of the river.

Christianity spread throughout the country after St. Mark introduced the religion to Egypt in AD 61. (Egyptian Christians are known as Copts; the word Copt means Egypt — derived from the Greek Aegyptius). The town near Babylon became predominantly Christian — the Holy Family are said to have stayed here when they fled to Egypt. Around AD 100 the Roman Emperor Trajan built a new fort, partly enclosed the town within its walls (this is the site of present-day Old Cairo) and adopted the name Babylon from the old fort. With the decline of Alexandria — Egypt's original capital of Christianity — Babylon became the main centre for Copts.

In 640, Amr, the Arab conqueror, founded the first Arab settlement at Fustat, next to Babylon. The town became the capital of medieval Egypt and one of the wealthiest cities in the oriental world.

Today the small district of Old Cairo retains a dominant Christian character although it is also the home of Jews and Muslims. The churches, museum and fascinating narrow, cobbled alleys make it one of the most interesting excursions in Cairo.

The Coptic Museum is important as it holds the greatest collection of Coptic art in the world, dating from AD 300 to AD 1000. Opening hours are from 9 am to 2 pm daily. Entrance: £E1. Guides are available at the entrance.

Abu Sergius is a church supposedly located on the spot where the Holy Family are said to have stayed during their flight. The church, dating back to the fifth century, is famous for its carvings of the Nativity.

The Synagogue, near Abu Sergius, was originally a Coptic church but was sold to the Jews in the ninth century.

El Muallakah, a church dedicated to the Virgin, is south east of Abu Sergius. Particularly significant are the twelfth-century pulpit and the coffers containing the bones of four saints.

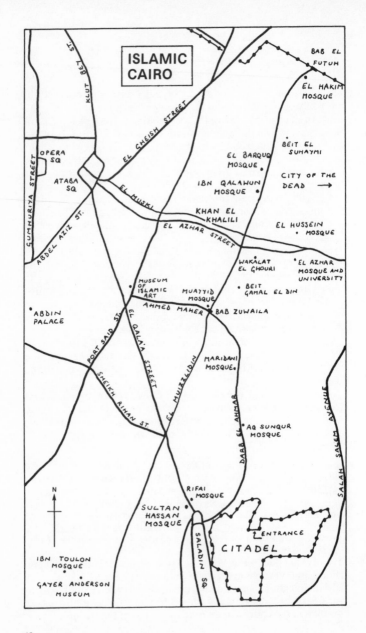

ISLAMIC CAIRO

BAB EL FUTUH

EL HAKIM MOSQUE

KLUT BEY ST.

EL GHEISH STREET

SUMHURIYA STREET

OPERA SQ

ATABA SQ

ABDEL AZIZ ST.

EL MUSKI

BEIT EL SUHAYMI

EL BARQUQ MOSQUE

CITY OF THE DEAD →

IBN QALAWUN MOSQUE

KHAN EL KHALILI

EL AZHAR STREET

EL HUSSEIN MOSQUE

WAKALAT EL GHOURI

EL AZHAR MOSQUE AND UNIVERSITY

MUSEUM OF ISLAMIC ART

MUAYYID MOSQUE

BEIT GAMAL EL DIN

ABDIN PALACE

AHMED MAHER

BAB ZUWAILA

PORT SAID ST.

EL QALA'A STREET

MARIDANI MOSQUE

SHEIKH RIHAN ST.

EL MUIZZLDIN

DARB EL AHMAR

AQ SUNQUR MOSQUE

SALAH SALEM AVENUE

N

RIFAI MOSQUE

SULTAN HASSAN MOSQUE

ENTRANCE

CITADEL

SALADIN SQ

IBN TOULON MOSQUE

GAYER ANDERSON MUSEUM

Amr Mosque is situated near the fortress walls in the Fustat area. It is said that God will answer prayers with special favours at this greatly revered mosque. It was constructed by Amr in AD 642 but was rebuilt several times during the following centuries. Today very little of the original mosque — the oldest in Egypt — remains.

The Nilometer, on the southern end of Roda Island, was first built in AD 716 by Osama bin Zed to gauge the height of the Nile waters.

To get to Old Cairo, take the suburban train, which leaves regularly from Bab El Louk station to Meri Gergis (a fifteen-minute ride). Alternatively there is a ferry service from the jetty opposite the TV building. Disembark at Meri Gergis on the east bank opposite Roda Island; from here Old Cairo is a ten-minute walk directly inland.

Islamic Cairo

The Tulinids (AD 868-906) and succeeding dynasties built their own quarters to the north east of Fustat, on the area now known as Islamic Cairo. A suggested route through this fascinating section of the city is from the Ibn Tulun Mosque via the Citadel along Darb el Ahmar and El Muizzlidin to the famous Kahn el Khalili Bazaars (see p.33).

From here, continue north to the city walls. You pass mosques (several of the more important charge an entrance fee; students are entitled to a discount) and lanes full of markets, craft shops and typical, traditional, Egyptian urban life. The route is approximately 4 km. Make several visits if you want to appreciate Islamic Cairo fully.

To get to Islamic Cairo take a No. 72 bus (going east) from Tahrir Square to the Citadel. Alternatively, it is 30-minute walk.

Many buses leave from 26th July Street to Al Azhar/Khan el Khalili. The 20 minute walk is easier.

Another interesting walk is from Khan El Khalili to Sharia Klut Bey and Rameses Square to the east. This area is less frequented by tourists and its domestic markets bustle with the atmosphere of everyday Cairo. The distance is about 2½ km as the crow flies.

Ibn Toulon Mosque was built in the latter half of the ninth century AD and is regarded as one of the most beautiful in Egypt. The size of the building, it covers over six acres, is particularly impressive and satisfies the Islamic objective of providing space in the courtyard for its adherents. It is said that a Christian designed the mosque.

Gayer Anderson House next to the Ibn Toulon Mosque, was the home of a late major who furnished his house with seventeenth-century Arabic furniture. It is now an interesting museum. It is open 8.30 am to 4 pm, Saturday to Thursday, 8.30 am to 11 am Friday.

The Sultan Hassan Mosque is colossal and is famous for its magnificent Islamic architecture. Built in the fourteenth century, it contained a school for the four different sects of Islam. The 85 m minaret is the second highest in Africa.

Rifai Mosque, opposite the Sultan Hassan Mosque, was built at the turn of the century for the late royal family.

The Citadel prominently situated on the slopes of the Mokattam hills and commanding a panoramic view of Cairo, is one of the city's most famous landmarks. It was built as a fortress by Saladin in AD 1180 from the stones of small pyramids. The ancient 100 m Joseph's Well is of particular interest as are the fourteenth-century An-Nasir Mosque, and the Mohammed Ali Mosque, which was designed by a European architect at the beginning of the last century. The most outstanding feature of this mosque is its huge central dome. It is sometimes known as the Alabaster Mosque because the walls are faced with alabaster. The tomb of Mohammed Ali is located here.

Aq Sunqur Mosque was built in the fourteenth century and restored in the seventeenth century. It is also known as the Blue Mosque because of the blue tiles on the walls.

The main feature of the fourteenth century **Al Maridani Mosque** is its ancient Egyptian red granite columns.

The fifteenth-century **Muayyid Mosque** is situated at Bab Zuwaila, one of the original gates to the Fatamid city of Cairo. The impressive bronze door was originally in the Sultan Hassan Mosque and the marble columns were taken from local churches. There is a fine view of Cairo from the minaret.

Beit Gamal El Din is a typical middle-class, seventeenth-century Arab House.

Wakalat El Ghouri, an interesting sixteenth century caravan-serrai, has tastefully been converted into a small complex of craft shops. It is open from 8 am to 2 pm, Saturday to Thursday, closed Friday.

El Azhar ('the splendid') **Mosque** and University is one of the best known mosques to visitors to Cairo. Dating from the tenth century, this is the earliest Fatimid Mosque in the city. Its university, regarded as the oldest in the world, has 20,000 students from all over the Muslim world.

Al Hussein Mosque is a central meeting point for Muslim worshippers — especially on the Prophet's birthday. It is named after the grandson of the Prophet and contains a Koran written by the son--in-law of Mohammed.

Ibn Qalawun Mosque was built by Sultan Qalawun in 1270 and included both a school and a hospital. The walls were originally covered with marble inlaid with mother of pearl, but sadly much of the mosque is now in a state of disrepair. The dome is the only one of its kind in Egypt.

El Barquq Mosque, dating from the 14th Century now in poor condition, is well known for its ceiling, windows, and the tomb of Barquq's daughter.

Beit El Suhaymi, in Darb El Asfar, is another example of a seventeenth to eighteenth century bourgeois Cairene dwelling.

El Hakim Mosque, situated in the shadows of the city walls, is an elegant eleventh century mosque in the process of renovation. Bab El Futah (Gate of the Conquest) and Bab El Nasr (Gate of Victory) stand next to the mosque.

The City of the Dead is a fascinating graveyard of Islamic Cairo. However, many mausoleums are now the residence of squatters. The Qaitbay Mausoleum, built in the fifteenth century, is one of the finest examples of Islamic architecture of its period.

The Museum of Islamic Art, situated in Ahmed Maher Square, houses a collection of exquisite Islamic art — probably the most valuable in the world.

Opening hours are (May to October) 9 am to 1 pm, Saturday to Thursday; 9 am to 12 noon, Friday; (November to April) 9 am to 4 pm, Saturday to Thursday; 9 am to 12 noon and 1.30 pm to 4 pm, Friday. Entrance: 50pt.

Other Places of Interest

Abdin Palace, at the end of Gumhuriya Street, is the grand former royal palace, completed in 1874. It is now government property and not open to the public.

Manial Palace, another extravagant royal palace, was built by Mohammed Ali on Roda Island. It is mainly a mixture of Persian and Ottoman styles. As well as being rich in Islamic objets d'art, the palace is famous for its mosaics. The Club Mediterranee is now situated in the palace gardens. Opening hours are 9 am to 1 pm daily.

The panoramic view from **Cairo Tower** (187m high), on Gezira Island, encompasses thousands of years of Egyptian history.

The Zoo, on the west bank along Giza Street, houses mainly Egyptian and Sudanese animals. It is open from 9 am to 5 pm daily.

Helwan, 24 km south of Cairo (take a train from Bab El Luq station) on the east bank, is a small spa town, popular with rheumatics because of its salt and sulphur springs. The necropolis of Sakkara is located opposite Helwan on the west bank.

Faiyum Oasis and **Lake Qarun,** situated 122 km south of Cairo, make a pleasant wooded retreat from the capital. Pharaohs of the 12th dynasty built their temples and pyramids here. Near the town of Faiyum are the ruins of Crocodilopolis where the Ptolemies worshipped Sobek, the water or crocodile god. Trains leave for Faiyum from Rameses Station in Cairo (change at El Wasta or Beni Suef), or take a bus from Tahrir Square.

Leaving Cairo

Rameses Station is in Rameses Square, 2¼ km north east of Tahrir Square. Buses travel between the station and Tahrir Square. Al Quolali, a short walk east of the station, is the terminal for buses and collective taxis to the Delta and the Suez Canal.

To Alexandria

By train

There are over a dozen trains a day, between 6.55 am and 11.30 pm, from Rameses Station. Not all have the full range of first-, second-, and third-class carriages. For the first- and second-class seats book your ticket at least a day in advance from the station. The two and a half hour journey passes through the fertile Delta region with its small traditional farmsteads and bustling towns.

By bus

The bus journey is — in complete contrast — via the desert route. The tarmac road (225 km) cuts the edge of the Libyan Desert. At halfway point is the rest house and a restaurant, where the bus usually stops for thirty minutes. Four Coptic monasteries, surrounded by desert and looking like something out of Beau Geste, are situated to the south of the rest house. Deir Suriani and Deir Amba Bishoi lie 12 km from the rest house; Deir Baramous is 10 km to their west. Deir Makaryus, further to the south, is 5 km from the main road — opposite the proposed Sadat City. Monks inhabit all the monasteries; visitors are welcome. You can take a jeep-taxi or hitch a lift from the rest house.

Many comfortable buses travel the desert route. They leave from Midan Tahrir (the back of the Hilton Hotel). Tickets are obtainable from the small kiosk a few doors to the right of the British Airways office in Tahrir Square (booking two hours in advance should be adequate.). Fares range from £E1.75 to £E3.50 depending on the class of bus. There are no student reductions. Duration: four hours. Collective taxis (via either the Delta or the Desert route) depart from Al Quolali, near Rameses Station.

To Suez, Port Said and Ismailia

Regular trains (from Rameses Station) and buses (from Al Quolali) leave for Suez, Port Said and Ismailia.

To Hurghada

Two buses a day depart from Ahmed Helmi (next to Rameses Station — east side). There is one at 7 am (£E3.65), another at 7.30 am (£E5). It's advisable to book a seat at least a day in advance. The journey takes six and a half hours.

You can also leave from Qena (62 km north of Luxor) by bus.

To Al Arish

A bus leaves for Al Arish daily at 10 am from Al Quolali (£E3.85). The journey takes six hours. Collective taxis depart from Rameses Square. Check at the Golden Hotel for further information about travel to Al Arish, and see the section 'Entering Egypt'.

To Luxor and Aswan

The main train services are follows:

Cairo Dep	0730	1900	1935
Luxor	1830	0606	0730
Aswan	2320	1000	

There are many other slower, cheaper services which provide 3rd class carriages. Sleeping compartments are available on the overnight services. Information on the new tourist services and full details of the train time-tables can be obtained from the Tourist Office, 5 Adly Street on the railway station in the Rameses Square.

A chapel inside Ambe Bishoi monastery, Wadi Natroun: About 10% of Egyptians are Christians (Copts). In recent years monasticism has revived and is now flourishing, particularly at the Wadi Natroum desert monasteries, between Cairo and Alexandria.

The seafront, Alexandria: Fishermen, in their traditional boats, collecting their nets.

4. Alexandria

Alexander the Great founded Alexandria in 332 BC with the intention of making it the central seaport of his Empire. However, he spent only six months in Egypt, and the construction of his city was left in the hands of his general, Ptolemy Soter (founder of the Greek Ptolemaic dynasty).

Alexandria rapidly became one of the wealthiest cities in the world: a library containing 500,000 volumes attracted scholars, lavish municipal buildings were erected, and most famous of all was the construction of the Pharos (lighthouse), where Fort Qait Bey stands today.

Although Julius Caesar entered Alexandria in 48 BC (when he first met Cleopatra), it was not until the reign of Augustus — after the deaths of Julius Caesar, Mark Antony and Cleopatra — that this seaport and the rest of Egypt really became part of the Roman Empire.

Christianity in Egypt evolved from St. Mark's preachings in Alexandria in AD 61. Christians suffered severe persecution, especially during the reign of Emperor Diocletian.

With the arrival of the Arabs in AD 640, Fustat (Cairo) developed as the capital and Alexandria's importance dwindled.

At the beginning of the last century Mohammed Ali revived the seaport with his extravagant development schemes. These attracted European entrepreneurs, and once again Alexandria became a wealthy, cosmopolitan city, divorced in character from the rest of Egypt. However, most of the foreigners left at the time of the Arab nationalist uprisings and Nasser's revolution.

Surprisingly little remains to be seen of Alexandria's colourful history. All the same, its atmosphere makes the city enchanting. Lawrence Durrell immortalised the romance of Alexandria in his 'Alexandria Quartet'. If you forget the recent and prosaic façade, an elegance and character is still to be found.

Where to stay

Alexandria's accommodation ranges from a youth hostel to the five-star Palastine at Montazah. In summer the many cheaper hotels are packed; in winter you'll have little trouble in finding a room and prices often drop. As in Cairo cheaper hotels are usually situated on one or two floors of a large house. If you can afford a little extra, it's worth paying for a seafront room in a hotel on the Corniche: the view of the Eastern harbour is magnificent.

The Youth Hostel (32 Port Said Street, Chatby — just beyond the eastern limit of the Eastern harbour) charges 60PT per night for a bed. The hostel is closed between 10 am and 12 noon.

St. Mark's College (at Chatby, between the tramlines and Pt Said Street) accommodates visitors when there's a shortage of beds in town for £E1.50 per night. Breakfast is included in the price.

The following are hotels where you can expect to pay under £E2 a night for a bed.

There are no single rooms at the **New Savoy** (148 26th July Street, off the Corniche — fourth floor); a double costs £E2.50. The **Besphore** is at 8 Orabi Street on Orabi Square. The **Lido** is at 1 Ibn Bassan Street, east of Ramla station, just beyond Ibrahim Mosque on the Corniche.

At the following hotels you can expect to pay between £E2 and £E4 a night for a bed.

The **Acropole** (Rue Gamal El Din Yasin, top floor) has recently been remodernized. **Philip House** (1 Ibn Bassan Street, on the Corniche, second floor — see the Lido above) has no single rooms and charges £E3 for a double.

The **Normandie** (8 Rue Gamal El Din Yasin, fourth floor) is on the Corniche in the next block to the famous Cecil Hotel. There are several hotels in the same building; this is the best.

The following establishments charge between £E4 and £E6 a night for a room.

Ailema (21 Rue Amin Fikri, seventh floor — near Ramla station) is under the same management as the Des Roses Hotel and the Oxford Pension in Cairo. It's clean and offers good value for money. Some rooms have private baths. On the floor above the Ailema is the **Hyde Park,** which offers much the same standard of accommodation.

The **Leroy** (25 Talaat Harb Street) is in the centre of town. There are attractive views of the sea from its restaurant. Some rooms have private baths.

The staff of the **Hotel Philip** (236 26th July Street/El Geish Avenue, fifth floor — ten minutes' walk from Ramla station heading east along the Corniche) claim they can speak seven languages between them. The hotel has recently been renovated. There is a disco, bar and restaurant. Some rooms have a private bath.

The **Admiral** (24 Rue Amin Fikri — near the Ailema Hotel) is modern with a gaudy interior and charges higher rates than the above hotels. The price however includes a private bath and breakfast. There is a disco, bar and restaurant.

A list of the more expensive hotels is available from the Tourist Office, in Zaghlul Square.

Where to eat

Mohammed Ahmed (17 Shaker Street, Ramla Square) is a very popular, cheap and unpretentious cafeteria that specializes in **ful** and **felafel.**

Gad has two establishments, in the centre of town, with the same menu as Mohammed Ahmed but at a higher price and with a fancier decor.

Cap d'Or (4 Adib Street, near Tahrir Square) is a cross between an American and a French bar, with a restaurant serving fish and kebabs (around £E2 for a main course).

Hosni (31 Safa Basha Street — off Ras El Tin) is a recommended small restaurant with a friendly atmosphere, situated in an old quarter of Alexandria. It serves kebabs and **kofta** (£E1.50 for a main course).

Ba'asm (near Hosni's) has much the same menu and atmosphere.

Alexandria is understandably well known for its seafood. At **Calithea,** a well known restaurant, (180 26th July Street), where you buy fish by weight (approximately £E5 a kilo).

Denis (Ibn Bassan Street) is another popular, modestly priced fish restaurant in the centre of town.

Zephyrion (in Abu Qir) is expensive but reputed to have the best seafood in Egypt.

Traverna Diamantakis (opposite Ramla station) is a recommended Greek restaurant.

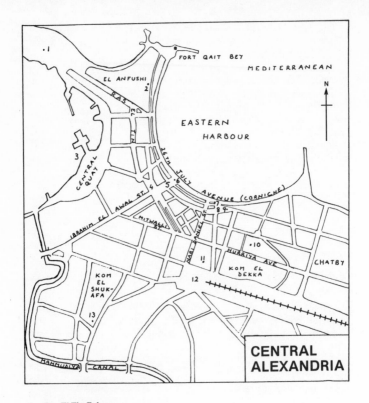

1   Ras El Tin Palace
2   Abul Abbas El Mursi Mosque
3   Passenger Ships' Harbour
4   Tahrir Square
5   Orabi Square
6   Tomb of the Unknown Soldier
7   Cecil Hotel
8   Zaghlul Square and the east end of Zaghlul Street
9   Ramla Square and Tram Station
10 Greco-Roman Museum
11 Roman Theatre
12 Gumhuriya Square and Masr (main) Railway Station
13 Pompeii's Pillar

The elegant tea houses are stubbornly resisting the Arabization of Alexandria. Four of the better known ones in the centre of town are **Athineos** (Ramla Square); **Delices** (Zaghlul Square); **Pastroudis** (39 Nasser Street — El Hurriya, Kom El Dekka), **Trianon** (Ramla Square). The **Brazilian Coffe Shop** in Zaghlul Street serves excellent coffee.

Shopping

There are several bazaars in the centre of town. From the north-east end of Tahrir Square along Rue de France (the start of Ras El Tin) up to Abul Abbas El Mursi Mosque is a market selling cotton, leather goods, gold, handicrafts and a general meat and vegetable market. There is an interesting section known as Zankh El Stat (the Street of the Crowded Ladies). Souk El Rateb, off El Nasr Street (the south-east corner of Tahrir Square) is a general bazaar and a meat and vegetable market. The more expensive, Western-style shopping area — a smaller version of Cairo's downtown — is in the centre of town around Zaghlul Street, Nebi Daniel Street, Talaat Harb Street and Hurriya Avenue.

Useful addresses

The Tourist Office is in Zaghlul Square.

The Passport Office is at 28 Talaat Harb Street. Visa Extensions are available here.

The Post Office is situated at the end of Chambre de Commerce Street. Telephones and Telegrams are at Ramla Station.

Foreign Banks in the city are Barclays (10 Fawatem Street — off Azurita Street), and Chase Manhatten (15 Doctor Ibrahim Abdel Sayed Street).

The British Consulate is at 3 Mena Street; tel: 47166. The **American Consulate** is at 15 Djabarti Street; tel: 28186.

Beaches

Alexandria is Egypt's summer resort and earlier this century was the playground of wealthy Europeans. During the season the town is teeming with holidaymakers, and though there are similarities with other Mediterranean resorts, Alexandria is not suffocated by cheap package tours and their gaudy accompaniments. A string of beaches runs along the city's eastern seafront up to Abu Qir, 29 km from the town centre. Some of the better beaches are Cleopatra, Glym, Stanley and Sidi Bish — all free. There is a small entrance fee to Muntazah and Mamura beaches. Seventeen kilometres to the west is the very popular Agamy beach (the no. 11 bus leaves from Orabi Square, and in summer collective taxis leave from outside Delices in Zaghlul Square).

What to do

The Greco-Roman Museum, Mataf Al Romani Street, is one of the city's main attractions. This interesting and well laid out museum mainly houses antiquities from the Greco-Roman period, thus filling the historical gap between the Pharaonic and Coptic eras. A comprehensive guide book with an introduction to the city's history is for sale at the entrance of the museum. The museum is open from 9 am to 3.30 pm, Saturday to Thursday; 9 am to 11.30 am and 1 pm to 3.30, Friday. Entrance:£E1.

The recently excavated **Roman Ampitheatre,** Kom El Dekka (north side of the square in front of the main railway station) is in excellent condition. The Christian graffiti on some of the stone slabs is particularly interesting. The amphitheatre is open from 9 am to 4 pm daily. Entrance: 25PT.

Pompey's Pillar, Amud El Sawari Street, Kom El Shukafa, in fact was erected by a Roman prefect in AD 302 to honour the Emperor Diocletian. The 28 m pillar stands alone on a low hill amongst the ruins of the Serapeum, a magnificent temple — once regarded as one of the world's most beautiful buildings — which held the statue of Serapis. Access to the pillar is from 9 am to 4 pm daily. Entrance: 50PT. To get there take a no. 9 bus from Zaghlul Square or take the interesting walk from the main railway station south west to Kom El Shukafa.

Turn right up the hill from the grounds of Pompey's Pillar and the **Catacombs of Kom El Shufaka** are on your right. They date from the end of the first century AD and are carved in three layers out of the rock and lie 30 m underground. The Catacombs are open from 9 am to 4 pm daily. Entrance: 50PT.

Other tombs in Alexandria are the **Necropolis of Anfoushi,** near Ras El Tin, which dates from the Ptolemaic era; the **Necropolis of Mustafa Pacha** (Moasker Street), which dates from the third century BC, and the **Necropolis of Chatby,** near the Youth Hostel.

Fort Qait Bey, situated at the northern tip of the harbour, was originally the site of a 177 m lighthouse, built by Ptolemy II in 279 BC. The lighthouse was known as the Pharos (after Pharos Island on which it was built) hence the French word **pharo,** and the Italian, **faro** — and was formerly regarded as one of the wonders of the world. It was destroyed by an earthquake in 1100. Some of the original stone blocks from the lighthouse were used in the construction of the recently renovated fifteen-th-century Fort Qait Bey. There is a small museum inside the fort with paintings depicting historical events in Egypt's history. It's open from 9 am to 1.30 pm, Saturday to Thursday; 9 am to 12 noon, Friday.

Caesareum was a lavish temple, begun by Cleopatra in honour of Mark Antony and later finished by Augustus. Today there is no evidence of the building, but its site is presumed to have been near the Eastern harbour. In 14 BC two obelisks were erected next to the entrance; at the end of the last century one of them was taken to London (and was erected on Victoria Embankment where it is popularly known as Cleopatra's needle), the other to New York.

The Aquarium (next to Fort Qait Bey) is no more than a couple of rows of tanks of small fish and is not very spectacular. It's open from 9 am to 2 pm daily.

Ras El Tin used to be the former Egyptian royal family's official Alexandrian residence. It later became a museum but is now closed to the public.

Muntazah Palace on the seafront to the east of Alexandria, was built by Khedive Abbas in 1892. Among the gardens of the estate is the first-class Palestine Hotel and the Zamelek Hotel (the former harem). Just to the east of the grounds is Mamura beach, one of the best in Alexandria. Opening hours for the gardens (the palace itself is closed to the public) are 9 am to 5 pm daily. Entrance fee: 50PT.

To get to the Palace and the beach take a train from the main station to Muntazah station, or catch the no. 20 bus on the Corniche at Zaghul Square.

Abu Qir (25 km) is where Nelson defeated the French fleet in 1798. It was also here, in 1799, that Napoleon, with nine thousand soldiers, defeated a Turkish army of 15,000 men. Abu Qir is now a small fishing port. The no. 28 bus from Orabi Square takes you to Abu Qir east of Alexandria.

To the west of Alexandria (distances are from the city centre) is **El Alamain** (105 km). There are the cemeteries of the soldiers who died in combat during the historic battle of the Second World War. Two buses a day leave from Orabi Square; the fare is £E2.50 and the journey takes two and a half hours. An early-morning train leaves from the main station.

The small port of **Marsa Matruh** (290 km) is a popular beach resort. Julius Caesar lived here for a short time with Cleopatra, and an offshore rock pool, known as Cleopatra's Bath, was named after the queen. There is a youth hostel and some fairly cheap hotels in the town. Collective taxis leave for Marsa Matruh from the square in front of the station; there is also a bus from Orabi Square and a main-line train. The trip takes four and a half hours.

Abu Mena (43 km) is 12 km south of Bahig and is the site of a Christian city named after a Roman soldier who converted to Christianity during the reign of Diocletian. The city grew around Mena's tomb and flourished in the fifth century, becoming an important place of pilgrimage. It fell into decay after the Arab invasion of Egypt, but today there are still remains of a monastery and several churches. A few kilometres from Bahig are the ruins of Abusir; these mark the site of a temple to Osiris dating from the third century BC. There is a main-line train to Bahig.

Leaving Alexandria

Frequent trains leave for **Cairo** from the main station (the journey takes two and a half hours). Buses leave from Zaghlul Square (four and a half hours) and follow either the Desert route, via Wadi Natroun, or the Delta route.

At least two buses a day leave from Zaghlul Square or Orabi Square to both **Suez** and **Port Said**. The journey costs £E3.50 and takes five and a half hours. Collective taxis leave from the square in front of the station.

5. Cairo to Luxor

The narrow green strips along the banks of the Nile are intensely cultivated. Fellahin practise their traditional methods of farming, irrigating the land with waterwheels, operated by a patient buffalo, to draw the Nile water which is then channelled into simple irrigation canals. Although the banks are heavily populated, their rural tranquillity is a pleasant contrast to the urban chaos of Cairo. Try to spend a few days amongst the villages along this stretch of river. Many relics of Egypt's ancient history stud the banks. Some of the more important towns and sites are mentioned below. (Distances are from Cairo.)

Minya (245 km) is an important market town, well known for its sugar factory. It's possible to make excursions from here to the rock tombs of Beni Hassan (268 km), on the east bank, opposite Abu Qurgas. Here, thirty-nine tombs of dignitaries from the 12th dynasty are hewn into the rock face. The wall paintings, depicting battle scenes and everyday life, are particularly noteworthy. Not far away is the graveyard for the cats which were dedicated to the cat goddess, Pekhet.

Mallawi (295 km) is an old Coptic centre.

Tell El Amarna (310 km) on the east bank (Deir Mawas is the nearest station — 6 km north), was founded by Amenophis, the heretic king of the 18th dynasty who rejected the Amun city of Thebes. The palace was to the south of the village of El Tell. Little remains of the city today. Tradition claims that the Holy Family lived at Nazali Ganub (330 km) for five years after they fled to Egypt.

Asyut (378 km) is the largest town in Upper Egypt and the starting point for the Ibrahim Canal which irrigates the provinces of Asyut, Minya and Beni Suef. This used to be the northern market town for the Darb El Arbain caravan route which linked Egypt to north-west Sudan. The bazaar is still an interesting feature. Cut into the hills on the edge of town are the tombs of the princes; these date from the 12th dynasty. The Soldiers' Tomb, with its illustrations of warriors, is particularly interesting. The hills provide a spectacular view of Asyut and the Nile.

Deir El Ahmar (Red Monastery) and **Deir El Abiad** (White Monastery) lie 5½ km north west and 5½ km south west respectively of the town of Sohag (480 km). Both were built in the ancient Egyptian style by Empress Helena in the fifth century. They got their names from the colour of their bricks.

Fourteen kilometres to the west of Balliana (522 km) lies the ancient site of **Abydos,** the most sacred place in Egypt during the Old Kingdom. It was the centre of the Osiris cult and one of the oldest temple sites in the history of Egypt. However, little remains of this period; but the more recent New Kingdom temples of Seti I and Rameses II are spectacular.

From **Qena** (610 km), on the east bank, a road branches off to Hurghada and the Red Sea. The most important site here is the well preserved **Dendera Temple** on the west side of the river. The magnificent temple was built in honour of the goddess Hathor between the second century BC and the second century AD. The names of the Roman emperors Domitian, Nerva and Trajan are inscribed on the gateway. On the south wall Cleopatra is depicted with her son Caesarion.

Oases

The region of the **Siwa Oasis,** near to the Libyan border, is closed to foreigners.

At least one bus a day leaves Asyut for **El Kharga** 230 kms to the West. The fare if £E1.50, the trip takes five hours. The cheapest hotel open to foreigners charges £E3 a night. The Ibsis Temple is 5 km north of the rest house.

One bus a day leaves El Kharga southbound for **Baris.** The fare is £E1, the trip takes three hours. Baris Hotel charges 75PT or sleep at the police station. The Dush Temple is 10 km to the south. It is advisable to bring your own food.

Several buses a week leave El Kharga for the town of Mut at the oasis of **Dakhla** (£E1.50, four hours). The hotel there charges £E1. Two buses a day leave from Mut, 15 km north to the village of El Qasr.

Transport to **Farafra** is very infrequent from Mut. The transport is fairly regular from Farafra to **Bahariya** and then on to Cairo.

6. Luxor

Luxor, built on the site of the ancient capital of Thebes, is beautifully located on the east bank of the Nile, 680 km south of the capital. Luxor and Cairo are the most important places to visit on the tourist itinerary. Although there is evidence of predynastic dwellings it was not until the 12th dynasty that Thebes became prominent. As the local god Amun became more important, so the city grew in size and wealth, until it reached its golden epoch in the 18th and 19th dynasties.

After the death of Rameses III in 1200 BC the priests gradually assumed power and eventually governed the country. However, a succession of foreign invasions by the Napatans, Assyrians, Persians, Ptolemies and Romans led to the decline of Thebes.

Where to stay

The number of hotels — of all standards — is increasing rapidly to cater for the tourist demand. Even so accommodation can be difficult to find in winter. Below are details of the cheaper hotels.

New Karnak on the left as you come out of the station charges £E3 for double room with bath, 60PT for a bed in a dormitory.

Radwan is next to the New Karnak. There are two to four beds to a room, and the charge per night is £E2 with breakfast.

To find **Negem El Din,** follow the road directly on the right of the station for a couple of minutes. It's a friendly, clean establishment and charges £E1.50 for a single, £E2.50 for a double. You can camp in the garden for 50PT.

Hatshepsut is about a fifteen minute walk south east of the town centre. It's quiet with a pleasant roof garden. They charge £E3 for a single, £E6 for a double with bath.

Amon on the left at the start of Mahatta Street (Station Street), at £E1.50 for a single, is good value.

The Nile at Luxor: Luxor, including Thebes on the west bank, is a mecca for tourists. However, a short distance out the town is a rural life continuing, apparently, as it has done for centuries.

The New Palace in Mohammed Farid Street (out of the station, take the first street on your left, walk about 200 m and it's the street on your left) charges £E1.50 for a bed.

The Sunshine Home is opposite the New Palace, with much the same prices and set up.

Horus opposite the mosque near the Avenue of Sphinx charges £E5.25 for double with bath.

The Youth Hostel in El Karnak Street (running parallel to the Nile, 200 m inland) is twenty minutes' north of the station. It has recently been modernized; beds are from 60PT.
You can camp, without charge, in the small grass area in front of the Luxor Hotel. There are no facilities.

There are a few hotels on the west bank on the way to the Valley of the Kings. The setting is serene and peaceful with none of the crowds of Luxor.

Memnon is opposite the Colossi of Memnon and charges £E2 for a single.

Sheik Ali is a popular hotel run by a well known character. A double room costs £E5.

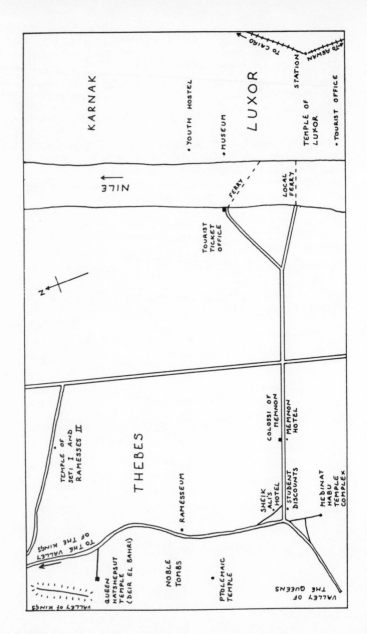

Getting around

El Karnak and the Temple of Luxor are located on the east bank. Across the Nile and several kilometres inland is the Valley of the Kings and other important tombs. The village of Sowaky, a couple of kilometres south east of the station, holds a camel market on Tuesday mornings. The sites are far apart and bicycles are a cheap and independent means of transport (you can take a bike on the ferry to the west bank). There are many bicycle-hire shops in the centre of Luxor; these charge around £E1.50 per day. You must leave an official document (say YHA card or driving licence as a deposit). A short ride out of town takes you into the lush and peaceful countryside.

Donkeys can be hired for around £E4 a day (including the services of the owner). This is a popular way to see the sites on the west bank.

The horse and buggy is Luxor's answer to the taxi. The Tourist Office has a list of the official fares. A return trip to Karnak from the town centre costs £E1.50.

The cheaper local ferry (5PT) leaves for the west bank from opposite the Mina Hotel on the Corniche.

Feluccas, elegant tall masted Egytian river boats, can be hired (with their owners) for excursions in the vicinity of Luxor — to Banana Island for example.

There are many tour operators, with offices in the centre of Luxor, who take visitors by bus to the various sites.

The Tourist Office is in the small shopping complex between the Temple of Luxor and the New Winter Palace Hotel.

The ferryman's house, Luxor.

What to do

A full range of guide books to the temples and tombs of Luxor, Karnak and Thebes is available from the tourist shops in Luxor.

Luxor Temple is in the town centre alongside the Nile. Amenophis III (18th dynasty) built the original temple to the god Amun, his wife Mut and their son Khonsa. Although Amenophis was the son of a Pharoah, his mother was not royal. By dedicating the temple to Amun he claimed divine ancestry and thus consolidated his power. Two obelisks used to stand at the entrance to the temples. In 1831 one was given to Louis Phillippe who re-erected it in the Place de la Concorde in Paris. Entrance: £E1.

Karnak Temple, 2½ km north of the town centre, is huge and well preserved. Dedicated to the god Amun, it is one of the most awe-inspiring and famous sites in Egypt. It was built by the Pharaohs of the 12th dynasty, but with additions during the later dynasties and Ptolemaic era. The Tourist Office provides a handout with a brief history of the temple. Entrance: £E2.

A **Son et Lumiere** relates the history of Thebes. This takes place at 6 pm daily. English performances take place on Monday, Wednesday and Saturday; French on Tuesday, Friday and Sunday; and Arabic and German on Thursday.

Luxor Museum, on the Corniche, 800 m downstream from the Luxor Temple, is a small, comprehensively arranged museum with relics from local sites. Entrance: £E1.

Thebes - West Bank

The nearest important tombs on the west bank are over 4 km inland from the jetty. There are taxis and coaches which cater for tourists, but it is cheaper to hire a bicycle in Luxor.

The main tombs require entrance fees which are all payable at the tourist ticket office on the west bank, not at the site itself. Student discounts are available from the bungalow approximately 4 km from the local ferry's jetty.

If you are cycling to the **Valley of the Kings** you can leave your bike at the Temple of Hatshepsut and climb over the hills behind the temple. Alternatively follow the road around the hills another 4 km.

It was in the Valley of the Kings that the pharoahs of the 18th, 19th and 20th dynasties dug their tombs out of the rock. So far sixty-four have been found; of those seventeen are open to the public. Three are particularly interesting.

The Tomb of Tutankhamun, the most famous and fortunately unnoticed by grave robbers, dates from the fourteenth century BC. **The Tomb of Seti I** includes beautiful, well preserved wall paintings and dates from the thirteenth century BC. In the **Tomb of Amenophis II,** dating from the fifteenth century BC, a special place was constructed for the burial so that the body could be hidden from the grave robbers. The ceiling depicts the heavens.

In the **Valley of the Nobles** three hundred tombs of dignitaries mainly from the 18th dynasty have so far been discovered. The wall paintings show scenes from everyday Egyptian life of this period. The tombs of Nakht, Ramose and Menena are among the most enchanting tombs in Thebes.

Queens, princes and princesses were buried in the **Valley of the Queens.** Only a few of the sixty or so tombs are open to the public. The tomb of Nefertari, wife of Rameses II, is the most interesting.

Hatshepsut Temple (Deir El Bahri) was built by Queen Hatshepsut in the fifteenth century B.C. and dedicated to the god Amun. Colonnades and terraces of this type are unknown elsewhere in ancient Egyptian architecture. Portraits and other evidence of the queen were destroyed by her stepson and successor, Thutmose III. In the seventh century Christians used the temple as a monastery.

Ramesseum is another large temple, dedicated to the god Amun by Rameses II in the thirteenth century BC. Near the entrance is the broken Rameses statue which stood 28 m and weighed 1,000 tons.

Deir El Medina was built by Ptolemy IV and dedicated to the goddess Hathor. The wall paintings are beautiful; it may be difficult to find someone to let you into the temple.

The Madinet Habu Complex comprises several temples and tombs, the most spectacular being the enormous and well preserved temple built by Rameses III in the twelfth century BC.

The Colossi of Memnon, famous 19 m high statues of Amenophis III, (18th dynasty) originally marked the entrance to the Temple of Amenophis.

Three important Ptolemaic temples lie between Luxor and Aswan. **Esna** was built by the Ptolemies and with additions by the Romans. The Roman emperor Trajan is depicted dressed as a Pharaoh. Inscriptions by Napoleon's soldiers are on the roof.

Edfu is regarded as one of the most perfect Egyptian temples. Built entirely in the Ptolemaic era, it is almost completely intact.

Kom Ombo is situated on a hill and was built and dedicated by the Ptolemies to the crocodile-headed Sobek and the hawk-headed Haroeris.

Hurghada, a small port and beach resort on the Red Sea coast, is becoming increasingly popular with tourists. Locals let rooms at reasonable prices. The offshore coral reefs are a great attraction.

Leaving Luxor

Several comfortable buses leave for **Aswan** each morning from TV Street (left out of the station, then approximately 400 m on the left in the same street as Seti Garden Hotel). The fare is £E2; the journey takes four hours.

Trains from Cairo to Aswan stop at Luxor. The fare from Luxor to Aswan is £E1.50 (second-class with air conditioning); the journey takes four hours.

Collective taxis leave from the square in El Karnak Street, a fifteen-minute walk north east from the station, and charge £E2 for the trip.

An extremely pleasant trip on the Nile is by **felucca.** It takes five days (three if you travel from Aswan to Luxor — downstream). An average boat holds six or seven people; and the fare is around £E15 per person — open to negotiation. You hire the **felucca,** with its owner, from the east bank of the Nile opposite the Winter Palace Hotel.

Several trains leave daily for **Cairo.** The express service takes eleven hours; the fare is £E4.40 (second class with air-conditioning).

To get to **Hurghada,** travel from Luxor to Qena by collective taxi (50PT). Taxis leave from the square in El Karnak Street. Three buses leave every morning from Qena for Hurghada (£E1.50, two and a half hours).

7 Aswan

Aswan, situated 900 km south of Cairo at the First Cataract, is Egypt's gateway to the African interior. The late Aga Khan owned a villa here and claimed that Aswan was one of the most beautiful places in the world. The town is now a popular winter resort.

Where to stay

The number of hotels in Aswan, like elsewhere in Egypt, does not meet the demand of the many tourists who arrive during the winter season. The following is a list of cheaper hotels.

Rosewan (first right out of the station, then first left) is cheap, clean and good value. It is in the process of renovation. A single room costs £E1.20.

Safa next to Rosewan, is of a slightly lower standard.

The Aswan Palace (left out of the station, approximately a kilometre down Market Street on the right) is clean, good value and popular with travellers. They charge £E1.30 for a single room.

The Continental, on the Corniche, approximately 1¾ km upstream from the station, was once a top hotel but has now lost its former splendour. There are no private rooms. It's usually full of young travellers who pay £E1 for a bed.

There are several other cheap hotels on or just off Market Street (the Amer, Khatab, Mores, Majestic), but they tend to be dirty and cramped.

The smaller, middle-range hotels start from £E6 for a single room with bath. **The Hathor, Philae, Abu Chieleb** and **Happi** Hotels are in the centre of town on or near the Corniche.

The Youth Hostel (out of the station, second turning on your left — Abtal El Tahrir Street — and a few metres on your right) has beds in a large dormitory from 60PT.

To get to the small camping garden go straight to the Corniche from the station, then a few minutes walk to the left. The overland truck tours to Sudan usually camp here.

Aswan: At the First Cataract, Aswan is Egypt's most southern town and its gateway to Africa. Sudanese merchants continue their long tradition of selling their goods in the main market. Today Aswan is a popular holiday resort with Egyptians.

What to do

To find the **Tourist Office,** walk to the Corniche from the station and turn left. The Office is just before the camping garden. The **Nile Navigation Corporation** is next door.

Feluccas ferry passengers to the islands and the west bank. The service leaves from opposite the Tourist Office.

Merchandise and handicrafts from the African countries to the south can be bought in the colourful market along **Market Street** and the area beyond.

The 2 km long **Elephantine Island** is an Aswan beauty spot and lies opposite the town centre. An interesting museum houses antiquities from the Aswan and Nubia regions. Nearby is a Nilometer constructed by the Romans; on the northern part of the island is the modern Oberoi Hotel.

The **Botanical Island** is just west of Elephantine Island. The gardens, founded by Lord Kitchener, contain a wide variety of tropical plants. It is a pleasant place to walk and relax.

The **Rock-hewn Tombs,** located on the west bank, date from the Old and Middle Kingdoms and are carved into the hillside.

The **Aga Khan Mausoleum,** an elegant structure, lies on the west bank opposite the Cataract Hotel. The Aga Khan died in 1957.

The **Monastery of St. Simeon** is situated in the desert about 1 km northwest of the Aga Khan Mausoleum. This fort-monastery, built in the eighth century but abandoned in the thirteenth century, is one of the oldest and best preserved Coptic buildings in existence.

Much of the ancient Egytians' building materials came from the **quarries** around Aswan. Particularly well known is the northern granite quarry just south of Aswan, where a 41 m obelisk lies unfinished.

Until recently the **Temple of Philae** was submerged during the Nile's annual flood. However, it was dismantled and re-erected on its present site on an island between the old dam and the high dam, 9 km south of Aswan. The earliest sections of the temples date from the fourth century BC; later additions were built by the Ptolemies and the Romans. The temple was dedicated to the worship of Isis. The fourteen-pillared Trajan's Kiosk is the best known structure on the island. To see the Temple, take a bus or train to El Shalla. Rowing boats cross to the island.

A few kilometres south of Aswan town is the **Aswan Dam,** built by the British in 1902. **The High Dam** is located 6½ km south of the Aswan dam. This impressive feat of modern technology was built by the Russians in order to control the Nile waters and irrigate the river banks. The dam is nearly 3½ km in length, over 100 m high, and the base about a kilometre thick. The Nile was first harnessed under this project in 1964. To get to the High Dam take a train from Aswan; it is about a ten minute walk from Aswan Harbour.

Abu Simbel, on the west bank of Lake Aswan (270 km south of Aswan) is one of the grandest temples of Egypt's ancient civilization. It was built by Rameses II in the 19th Dynasty (between 1300 and 1233 BC) in honour of the gods Path, Amun and Harakte. The entrance to the temple is dominated by four colossal 22 m statues of Rameses II. Access to the temple is difficult unless you go with an official tour company; contact the Tourist Office for information on excursions.

Leaving Aswan

For the south there are at least two trains a day making the 45 minute journey passing the High Dam and terminating at the Aswan Harbour Station.

For the north one has various options:-
Buses: There are several buses a day to Luxor. These, and the **collective taxis** both depart from behind the Abu Simbel Hotel in Abtal Tahrir Street.

Trains: There are several trains via Luxor to Cairo each day.

Planes: There is a scheduled service operating to Cairo.

(The route from Aswan Harbour to Sudan continues on p.122.)

Aswan-Wadi Halfa ferry: Although the ferry from Aswan to Wadi Halfa is crowded the two day journey is quiet, pleasant and relaxing.

74

Part 2
Sudan

"Perhaps to Englishmen — half savage still on the pinnacle of their civilization — the very charm of the land lies in it's empty barbarism. There is space in Sudan.... You are a naked man, facing naked nature. I do not believe that any one of us who come home whole will think, from our easy chairs, unkindly of Sudan."

From **With Kitchener to Khartum** by G.W. Stevens, a war correspondent with Kitchener at the end of the last century.

Contents: Sudan

Basic Information

This map shows the railways and main rivers of Sudan. The 'blocks' across the Nile numbered 2-6 indicate the position of the cataracts.

78

Sudan — Basic Information

Area: 2,505,813 sq. km. Sudan, the largest country in Africa, is bordered by Egypt, Libya, Chad, CAR, Zaire, Uganda, Kenya and Ethiopia.

Population: 17,290,000: Khartoum 334,000, Omdurman 300,000, Khartoum North 151,000, Pt Sudan 133,000, Juba 57,000. Twenty-five per cent of population lives in the Blue Nile and Khartoum provinces (which cover 6.5% of the total land area). Fifty per cent of the population is under twenty years old; ninety per cent is rural.

Provinces: Sudan comprises the provinces of Bhar El Ghazal, Blue Nile, Darfur, Equatoria, Kassala, Khartoum, Kordofan, Northern, Red Sea, and Upper Nile.

Language: Arabic is the official language, although almost a hundred different dialects are spoken throughout the country. English is widely spoken in the South.

Religion: Muslim: seventy-two per cent; Christianity: five per cent; traditional: twenty per cent.

Government: Sudan is a republic with a 250-member Assembly; the Sudan Socialist Union (SSU), headed by President Jafaar Nimeiri, is the only party.

Economy: Dealt with on p. 83.

Income: (per capita): $230(1976).

Time: GMT + 2 hours.

Electricity: 240 volts single-phase AC.

1 The Country

At face value Sudan has little to attract the tourist: mile after mile of sunbaked desert in the north, tropical vegetation flooded by rain for most of the year in the south. It lacks the antiquity or artistic magnificence of Egypt, and — except for a few places — the scenic picture-postcard beauty of Kenya. But when comparing Sudan with these two countries, travellers will invariably claim that it leaves them with the most lasting and favourable impression. Travelling to remote areas, contact with people almost unaffected by the West, experiencing the country's vastness (Sudan is ten times the size of Britain) with its gradual transition from the Arab cultures in the north to the 'True African' Black cultures in the south, and, of course, the magic of the Nile are all unforgettable. However, it is the open warmth, gentleness and sincerity of the Sudanese which have a far more memorable effect on any visitor to the country.

Geography

The Rivers

It's debatable whether the Nile or the Amazon is the world's longest river. However, one thing is certain, nowhere else are two countries so dependent on the regular flow of a river as Egypt and Sudan on the 6,500 km Nile.

Lake Victoria is the recognized source of the White Nile, although surprisingly it's not from here that the river gets most of its water but from the numerous tributaries between Lake Albert and Mongalla (between Juba and Bor) in south Sudan. At Bor the Nile enters a massive clay plain and overflows into channels that form the Sudd — a vast 7,500 sq. km swamp. From the Sudd the milky brown waters of the White Nile, regenerated by the River Sobat at Malakal, slug on to Khartoum where they are met by the Blue Nile.

During the rains the Blue Nile, rising from Lake Tana in the Ethiopian highlands, and its tributaries, the Dinder and Rahad, account for seventy per cent of the river's water below Khartoum. In the dry season the position is reversed with the ever consistant White Nile contributing eighty per cent.

There are no real tributaries between Khartoum and the Mediterranean except for the seasonal River Atbara, which between June and September becomes a raging torrent carrying more soil (drainage is from the Ethiopian highlands) into the Nile than any other of the great river's tributaries. The Nile forms a large S as it snakes a 1,450 km course from the capital northwards through semi desert and desert to Lake Aswan.

Desert

A line running east to west across the country through Atbara forms the approximate southern limits of the desert. This stone and desert region up to the Egyptian border (twenty four per cent of the country) is sparsely habited, except for the coast and settlements that desperately hug the banks of the Nile. In some areas rain may not fall for several years on end.

In the Nubian Desert, to the east of the river, nomads such as the Bisharin eke out an existance. To the west, in the harsh Libyan desert, the Kababish and a few other tribes with their camels and goats wander great distances in search of **gizu** (a type of grass for grazing). There are the occasional oases like Selima and Al Altrun on the Darb Al Arbain (a centuries-old caravan route which runs from El Fasher in Darfur Province to Asyut in Egypt), but it is the towns along the Nile that act as the main market for the nomads.

The Four Mountain Regions

The **Red Sea Hills,** running parallel to the coast just behind Pt Sudan, are the home of groups of the Beja tribe who graze and cultivate wherever possible. North of Sinkat there's little vegetation; to the south it's greener with beauty spots such as lush, cool Erkowit. The highest peak is Jebel Oda, at 2,265 m, some 100 km north of Pt Sudan.

Near the western border in Darfur Province is the fertile region of **Jebel Marra,** home of the Fur, which boasts some of the country's richest orchards (mangoes, guavas, citrus fruits). The mountain range, of volcanic origin, is the highest in North Sudan (Jebel Gimbala is 3,071 m) and forms a watershed between the Nile and Lake Chad Basin.

The scattered granite hills of the **Nuba Mountains** rise 1,000 m above the plains of South Kordofan. The Nuba cultivate terraces on the seasonally watered slopes.

The **Immatong and Dongotona Mountains** are beautiful rain forest hills on the Ugandan border. The Immatongs are the highest mountains in Sudan (Mt Kinyeti is 3,170 m) and their slopes are cultivated by various tribes.

81

Climate

Sudan lies entirely within the tropics and for the most part has a tropical continental climate in which two winds play an important part: the Northerlies bring cool, dry weather in winter and heat in the summer; the Southerlies carry rain from the south in January and reach their northern extreme in August.

The Northerlies dominate the desert regions of the dry north; temperatures are high and rainfall low, 0.1 mm per annum. Old Wadi Halfa once notched up a record as the hottest town in the world at 52.5°C and has also recorded Sudan's coldest temperature, -2°C.

As you move south the Southerlies become more influential. In Khartoum (average annual rainfall is 175mm) the rainy season occupies July and August; in the humid south, with its equatorial rainfall, it lasts from April to November, with an average annual rainfall of 1,250 mm. Over half the country's rain falls in August — the wettest month for most of the Sudan.

The climate of the Red Sea coast differs from the rest of Sudan; rain can fall throughout the year but it has a distinct season in November and December. The climate of the mountain regions and the Sudd has slight local variations.

The hottest, driest period throughout the country is just before the Rains. Haboobs (sand/dust storms like the siroccos) are common in the north; some say they can be so dense that you can't see an arm's length in front of you. After the Rains Sudan is cool and green — from October or November onwards is the best time to visit the country. From March the heat picks up again.

Temperatures

This chart shows average temperatures during the hottest and coolest months.

	Min.	Max.		Min.	Max	
Abu Hamed	27°C	43°C	June	13°C	28°C	January
Pt Sudan	30°C	41°C	August	19°C	26°C	February
Khartoum	27°C	42°C	June	16°C	31°C	January
Nyala	23°C	38°C	May	16°C	31°C	January
Kosti	25°C	40°C	May	17°C	33°C	January
Kassala	25°C	41°C	May	16°C	34°C	January
Malakal	23°C	38°C	April	22°C	30°C	August
Juba	23°C	37°C	March	20°C	30°C	August

The climate is characterised by a low level of humidity in the north and a high level in the south.

Economy

The country's agricultural and pastoral economy accounts for eighty per cent of the labour force and ninety per cent of the exports (of which fifty-three per cent is cotton and fourteen per cent groundnuts). Sudan is also one of the world's leading producers of gum arabic and sesame. Industry is essentially agro-industrial: mainly the processing of foods, textiles and leather.

Only ten per cent of Sudan's potential arable land is actually farmed, and in the mid-1970s plans were drawn up to cultivate its lands to make the country the bread-basket of the Arab world. The idea was an attractive one: The West could export their technology; the Arabs could invest their money — a budget of six billion dollars over the next ten years was proposed; and the Sudanese could develop their lands. However, the country was too eager to develop quickly and its economy, hindered by a poor transport system, couldn't cope with the schemes. As imports increased so did the national debt, and in 1978 the government turned to the IMF for support. One of Sudan's solutions was to cut back on development expenditure. The intention was to complete unfinished projects — in particular new roads — and get them in full swing before embarking on fresh ventures.

Development Projects

Most of the money for development is being put towards improving the infrastructure and increasing the agricultural output. Among the most enterprising projects are the Rahad irrigation scheme, the Jonglei canal scheme and the Kenana sugar plant.

The former involves the utilisation of the Blue Nile waters stored at the Roseires dam to irrigate 820,000 **feddans** (one feddan equals approximately one acre), primarily in the Gezira region — a vast plain south of Khartoum, between the White and Blue Niles.

The 380 km Jonglei canal is to drain part of the Sudd and reclaim four million cubic metres of water lost annually through evaporation.

The Kenana sugar plant, near Kosti, is one of the largest in the world. It opened earlier in 1981 and is expected to have an annual output of 330,000 tonnes.

History

Ancient Sudan

Sudan's history has always been closely linked to that of Egypt. The Ancient Egyptians referred to the lands to their south as **bilad al sudan** (land of the blacks). From the time of the Old Kingdom Egypt sent sporadic raiding and trading parties into North Sudan; they would return with ivory, ebony and slaves.

12th Dynasty. Egyptians build fortresses between the First and Second Cataracts in order to supervise the area's gold resources. A fort at Semna (Second Cataract) protects Egypt's southern border.

The Nubian kingdom of Kush develops around the trading town of Kerma (Third Cataract).

At the end of this dynasty the Egyptians were forced to retire because of an invasion to their north.

18th dynasty. The Egyptians reconquer Sudan and push the border south to the Fourth Cataract. This time they bring with them artisans and craftsmen, establish towns (for example Kawa and Amara) and erect temples such as the one at Jebel Barkal (1450 BC). Formerly, the Kushites were depicted in art as being under Egyptian domination, now they are shown exchanging gifts.

Late Dynastic Period. Egypt loses its grip on Sudan. By 1000 BC Kush is an independent state. A new and powerful kingdom — similar to the Amun state at Thebes — extends from Aswan to the Blue Nile region with its capital at Napata (present-day Merowe).

Napatan Age. The great Napatan King, Piankhi, conquers the whole of Egypt. He rebuilds the temple at
721 BC Jebel Barkal and revives the custom of pyramid burials.

Piankhi's successor, Shabaka, moves the capital to Thebes and establishes the Egyptian's 25th dynasty.

654 BC Shabaka's son, Taharqa the Great, is pushed back to Napata by Assyrian invaders entering northern Egypt.

Relations between Napata and Egypt deteriorate and Napata gradually declines. Simultaneously, Meroe (north of present-day Shendi), a fertile area and a cross-

580 BC roads for caravans, grows, slowly dwarfing the capital.

For a while both towns have a king. Eventually, Meroe
350 BC becomes the capital and heralds the Meriotic age.

Meriotic Age.   The Egyptian influence dwindles.
Meroe's territory expands (for some time it stretches
from the First Cataract to the Upper Nile region).
Independent of foreign rulers it flourishes and temples
and pyramids are erected.   However, there are also
influences by or from other civilizations — the Romans,
Greeks and Persians — as can be seen from the temples
at Nagaa and Musawareret.

A Meriotic form of hieroglypics evolves — as yet
undeciphered.   It is now thought that iron-smelting
spread from here to other parts of Africa.

23 BC The Romans in Egypt sack Napata and seriously
weaken the northern Meriotic kingdom.   A gradual
decline follows, accelerated by attacks from the nomadic Blemmya, ancestors of the Beja.

AD 350 Finally, the Abyssinians destroy Meroe.

At present little is known about ancient history of the South.

Christian Era

The history of the two hundred years following the fall of Meroe
is vague.   It is known that Christians fleeing persecution in
Egypt first reached Nubia in the fourth century.

6th century.   Justinian, Emperor of Constantinople,
and his wife Theodora send missionaries to Nubia.

The Church of Sudan becomes linked to the Patriarch in
Alexandria.

Two Nubian kingdoms emerge: Makuria, from the First
to the Fourth Cataract, with a capital at Old Dongola;
and Alwa, from the Fourth Cataract to near present-day
Sennar, with a capital at Soba (on the Blue Nile, 16 km
south east of Khartoum).   Both are prosperous.

14th century. Makuria slowly declines. The Arabs from Egypt gradually take over power.

1505 Alwa is destroyed by the Qawasma Arabs from the north and the negro Funj from the south

The Funj and Fur Kingdoms

The Funj Kingdom (also known as the Black Sultanate) stretched south to Sennar from the sixth Cataract.

16th century. Two states are formed: one under King Dunkas of the Funj, and the other under Abdullah Jemma, sheikh of the Qawasma. The two states consolidate with a fairly centralized government at Sennar.

Muslim missionaries visit Sennar, and for the first time Islam has a real influence in Sudan.

18th century. The Funj era reaches its height after the king's victories in the Abyssinian and Kordofan wars.

1760s Internal skirmishes cause the king to become no more than a puppet in the hands of rival groups. The Black Sultanate declines until the arrival of the Egyptians in 1821

The Fur Kingdom existed in Darfur at the same time as that of the Funj. Its eastern border was somewhere in Kordofan — the exact position depended on the outcome of the wars with the Funj.

mid-17th century. King Sulayman Selonj unites the Fur under the banner of Islam.

The Sultanate of Fur thrives for 250 years. Except for a short period in the 19th century, it maintains reasonable independence until 1916, when it is overthrown by the Anglo-Egyptian forces.

Turko-Egyptian Colonization

1805 Muhammed Ali overthrows the Mameluke rule in Egypt and establishes his own powerful government beneath the Ottoman umbrella.

1821 Muhammed Ali sends armies south into Sudan in search of gold and slaves. The Funj kingdom falls to the invaders.

1823 Mek Nimr, a local chief from Shendi, kills Muhammed Ali's son, Ismail, while he is feasting. Muhammed Ali's son-in-law, Deftarder, moves east from Kordofan to avenge this murder. Some sources claim that he killed 30,000 Sudanese.

The Turko-Egyptian colonizers (called 'Turks' because of their Ottoman links) establish a central government.

1849 Muhammed Ali dies.

1849 His successors, Abbass and then Muhammed Said,
  63 neglect their colony. Officials posted in Sudan regard their term of office as a punishment because of the harsh conditions in the country. They resort to corruption and exploitation — usually at the expense of the Sudanese.
The profitable slave trade attracts Europeans — 'the scum and shame of Europe', in the words of Brehm, a contemporary German traveller.

1863 Ismail Pasha succeeds Muhammed Said as Khedive of Egypt and employs Samuel Baker to suppress slavery in the south and establish Egyptian authority — both with limited success.

1877 Later, Charles George Gordon is sent and wins the confidence of the natives.

Charles Gordon is made Governor General of Sudan and does much to end slavery and establish administrative order.

1879 Ismail is deposed. Gordon resigns and leaves behind him a far from stable country.

The Mahdiya

The tribes of Sudan had never been united, but now they shared a hatred for the colonial Turks. The time was ripe for the Mahdi ('one guided by God'), Mohammed Ahmed. He was born in 1844 near Dongola and moved south to join various religious fraternities at Aba Island (near present-day Kosti).

1881 Mohammed Ahmed declares himself Mahdi. He wants to return to a simple pure form of Islam, unite under one flag, and establish a religious society. At first the Egyptians do not treat the uprising seriously.

1882 The British occupy Egypt.

1883 The Mahdi declares a **jihad** (holy war) and successfully besieges El Obeid, suppresses an Egyptian army under William Hicks, an English colonel, and gains control of Kordofan.

In the west Mohammed Ahmed's followers enjoy successive victories; most of the east falls to the sword of Osman Digna, the Mahdist general.

1884 British Prime Minister Gladstone sends General Charles Gordon to withdraw the Egyptian army from Sudan. Soon after his arrival the Mahdists besiege Khartoum.

1885 On 26th January Khartoum falls and Gordon is killed. The Egyptian rule is over.

Six months later the Mahdi dies of typhus. He is succeeded by Khalifa Abdullah, his right-hand man, who rules the Mahdist state for the remainder of its thirteen years. This period is beset by internal rebellions, wars against Abyssinia and Egypt, a smallpox epidemic and a famine. The state is weakened and the population drops about four million.

1896 The Anglo-Egyptian army under Sir Herbert Kitchener moves south from Egypt, building a railway as they progress. This proves disastrous for the Mahdists. Winston Churchill, then a war correspondent, wrote: 'Fighting the Dervish (refering to the Mahdists) was primarily a matter of transport. The Khalifa was conquered on the railway.'

1898 Kitchener reaches Omdurman at the end of August, having defeated the enemy on the way.

On 3rd September, the Mahdists are decimated at the Battle of Omdurman. Kitchener then moves on to Khartoum and hoists both the Union Jack and the Egyptian flag over Gordon's ruined palace. This marks the beginning of the Anglo-Egyptian condominium (joint rule over the state's affairs).

By the end of 1899, Khalifa and other important figures are dead and the Mahdiya comes to an end.

The Condominium and Independence

Under the Condominium Sudan gained separate political status. Although Britain and Egypt shared control, Britain was more powerful.

1899- The British set about pacifying the country and estab-
1920 lishing an administration. Communications improve; an export economy is created; cotton projects (especially in the Gezira region) become the backbone of Sudan's economy. Courts of Justice, medical centres and schools are established.

1920s A Western-educated elite graduates from the Gordon Memorial College; many resent the Condominium.

1924 The White Flag League, aimed at driving out the British is formed.

Sir Lee Stack, Governor General, is assassinated.

late 1930s The Graduates General Congress make moves towards
and 1940s gaining independence.

The Congress divides into the Ashiqqa (Blood Brothers) party, who favour the establishment of a democratic Sudanese government in union with Egypt, and the Umma party, who reject such ties. To gain support, the parties link themselves to powerful religious orders: the Ashiqqa to the Khatmiya and the Umma to the Ansar. These parties are the foundation of the future democratic parliamentary system.

The British allow the nationalists more power within the government.

1952 The Naguib-Nasser **coup d'état** takes place in Egypt. The British persuade and the new Egyptian government agrees that Sudan should be granted independence.

1955 The beginning of the North-South civil war.

1956 On 1st January Sudan becomes an independent republic with an elected representative parliament.

1958 General Ibrahim Abboud stages a military coup, overthrows a disunited government and gains control.

1964 The initial popularity of the new regime wanes because of Abboud's inability to end the North-South conflict. This leads to the October Revolution and Abboud's abdication.

1965 After a short period of political uncertainty, a new cabinet — comprising the Umma Party, the National Unionist Party and the Muslim Brotherhood — is formed. However, the North-South civil war continues.

1969 Colonel Jafaar Nimeiri leads a successful military coup on 25th May.

Nimeiri establishes a new government and pronounces Sudan 'democratic, socialist and non aligned'. He opposes influential sects, claiming the struggle against religious fanaticism is a social and economic necessity

1971 The Communist Party attempts a **coup d'état.**

1972 The Addis Ababa Agreement ends the North-South war. To date this is Nimeiri's greatest achievement.

The Peoples of Sudan

With the present vogue to experience 'Real Africa' before it vanishes, Westerners ranging from the casual traveller to the sophisticated film-maker are being pulled by the aura of the untouched tribes of Sudan. There are still many areas of the country, however, which are hardly visited by foreigners.

Culturally Sudan is extremely varied with some six hundred tribal groups: the following is a brief background on the main ethnic groups of the country.

Northern Sudan

Before the arrival of the Arabs the Northern desert of Sudan was dominated by the Nubians, who mainly farmed along the banks of the Nile, and the nomadic Beja. With the coming of the Arabs both groups converted to Islam, though the Beja retained much of their independence — a characteristic still typical today. In Darfur the nomadic Zaghawa was a third smaller group.

Nubians

Originally the Nubians were Nilotes, who migrated from the south and eventually formed much of the population in the Kingdom of Meroe. They are the most negroid of the northern Sudanese, though the intermixing with the Arabs over the centuries has resulted in their reddish-brown skin colour.

Today the bulk of them live in Nubia: for instance, the Danagla and the Maha (both with vertical scars on their cheeks), and the Shaiqiya (with three horizontal scars on their cheek). It's thought that the Nubians originally scarred themselves so as to be distinguished from the negroes of the South.

There are substantial Nubian settlements in the Nuba mountains (the Nubians differ from the Nuba people) and in Darfur. President Nimeiri is a Nubian, so was the Mahdi.

Beja

The Beja are the 'Fuzzy Wuzzies' that Rudyard Kipling wrote about: short, with dark-brown wavy hair and Caucasian features — in fact, resembling the Ancient Egyptians. It is believed that they have lived in their present territory for the last six thousand years.

Most Beja belong to the three Bedawiya-speaking tribes: the Bisharin, the Amarar and the Haddendowa. In the north, on the Egyptian border, there are the Ababda, who have mixed with Arabs, in the south, on the Eritrean border are the Beni Amer. The Beja are almost exclusively pastoralists and live in tents in groups of three to four families, moving about in search of grazing especially around the Red Sea area.

Zaghawa

The Zaghawa — semi-nomadic Saharan negroes — live in the deserts of north Darfur. They are nominally Arabized though still practise their own customs and have little contact with the rest of Sudan.

Central Region

The vast central belt running across the country is predominantly Arab, though many West Africans (ten per cent of the North's population is West African) and Southerners have moved here in search of jobs.

Arabs

Apparently no tribe in Sudan can claim a pure Arab pedigree; all the same traditionally most profess descent from one of two genealogies: the Juhayna and the Jaaliin. The Juhayna incorporate nearly all the nomads and believe the Kahtanites, aristocrats from Saudi Arabia, are their ancestors.

The Baggara, the largest tribal group, has a population of six million and includes such tribes as the Rizaygat, the Taisha (the Khalifa was a Taishi) and the Selima. Being so near the south the Baggara not only interbred with the negroes (which can be seen by their appearance) but were also some of the most notorious slave traders in the last century. The Baggara are mainly cattle herders, but to their north is a sub-group of the tribe known as the Jamala. These are the least negroid of Sudan's Arabs and include tribes such as the Kababish and Shukriyyah who still practise the traditional camel nomadism. However, there is a growing trend away from camels to cattle and, where possible, the cultivation of crops.

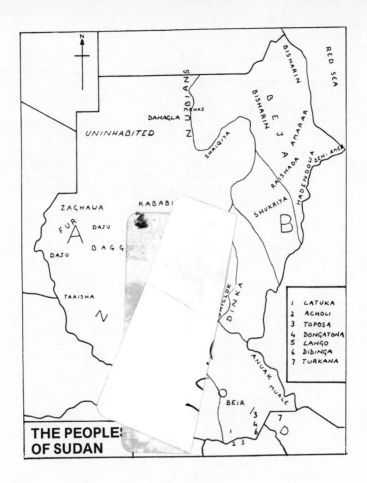

THE PEOPLES
OF SUDAN

N

1	LATUKA
2	ACHOLI
3	TOPOSA
4	DONGATONA
5	LANGO
6	DIDINGA
7	TURKANA

RED SEA

BISHARIN

BEJA

DISHARIN

AMARAR

RAISHADA

HADENDOWA

BENI AMER

SHUKRIYA

B

NUBIANS

MAHAS

DANAGLA

SHAIQIYA

UNINHABITED

ZAGHAWA

KABABI

FUR

A

DAJU

DAJU

BAGG

TAAISHA

N

SHILLUK

DINKA

ANUAK

MURLE

BEIR

3
4
6
1
2 S

D

7

The Jaaliin trace their descent back to Al-Abbas, the uncle of the Prophet. The term refers either to the riverside inhabitants between Dongola and Sabaloga or, more specifically, to those between Atbara and Sabaloga, who are characterized by an H-shaped scar on their cheek. Nowadays they tend to be settled farmers.

There are also Arabs who claim strong links with Arabia: for example, the Kawahla and the Raishada, who have been in the Sudan only 130 years.

Fur

The Province of Darfur is named after the Fur, negroes who live around Jebel Marra.

From the seventeenth century until 1916 Darfur had its own independent royal family of Arab and negro origin. The Fur are Muslim, though they retain many unique traditional customs.

Daju

The Daju are negroes who probably originated from the Upper Nile and dominated the Darfur region before the Fur. The group is dying out, though small enclaves still exist in south-west Darfur and the western Nuba mountains.

Nuba

Their dramatic and colourful rituals have made the Nuba subjects of several glossy coffee-table books. They are negroes: most people believe they either originated from West Africa or migrated from the south. They settled throughout Kordofan and the Nile Valley before being pushed back into the Nuba mountains by Arab colonization. Only recently have some returned to the plains of Kordofan.

The Nuba seem to have little tribal unity and live in small groups, cultivating terraces on the side of the hills and coming together only for special occasions. The language of the Nuba seems unrelated to any other tongue.

Southern Sudan

Ninety-eight per cent of the Southern population is negro, ethnically far more closely related to peoples of the countries to their south, east and west than to the northern Sudanese. The two main ethnic groups of the south are the Nilotes and the Sudanic people.

Nilotes

All the Nilotes of south Sudan settled in their present territories in the last thousand years. They originally migrated north from around Lake Turkana in Kenya, absorbing existing tribes and settling in the region of the Upper Nile — from where their name is derived. Today the Nilotes of northern Sudan (for example, the Nubians) have little in common with the southern Nilotes.

The Dinka, Nuer and Shilluk are among the better-known Southern tribes: tall (6 ft 6 ins is very common), lanky and very black; the Dinka and Nuer are essentially pastoralists, though many are now settled farmers.

Dinka

The Dinka live in a 350,000 sq km area and are the largest of the Nilote groups, comprising of ten per cent of Sudan's population. Their names, rituals and nearly all aspects of their life have associations with cattle. In the last hundred and fifty years the Nuer have established themselves on Dinka land, subsequently dividing the northern Pedang Dinka from the main southern body. The Dinka are particularly famous for their songs (invariably about cattle) and their dancing, in which they jump as high as they can in 'pogo' fashion. The scar which runs across the lower part of their forehead is 'beaded' by filling the incisions with ashes.

Nuer

The Nuer are closely related to the Dinka, but whereas the Dinka are divided into many groups the Nuer are more compact and independent. They scar their forehead with several lines and sometimes plug their lower lip, ears and nose with wooden ornaments.

Shilluk

The Shilluk have lived on their present territory since they defeated outposts of the Funj kingdom in the sixteenth century. They are a tight farming community moving from the banks of the Nile to slightly higher ground only during the Rains. The Shilluk are particularly famous for their divine kingship (see P. 100). They scar themselves in the same way as the Dinka and are known for their elaborate hairstyles.

Lou

The term Lou denotes people with a particular pattern of migration. They live in Sudan, Uganda and Kenya. In Sudan, the Acholi are probably the best-known group.

Toposa

The semi-nomadic Toposa live in the area around the Torit to Kapoeta road. They have a reputation for fighting at the slightest provocation.

Anuak

The Anuak straddle the Sudanese/Ethiopian border. They farm mainly around the River Sobat, though they have villages further to the south. There is a history of fighting between the Anuak and Nuer.

The Didinga, Beir and Murle

These tribes have little contact with each other, but they are related through a common language. The Didinga farm on the slopes of the mountains named after them; the Murle trade along the Ethiopian border, and the Beir farm on the Pibor River.

The Bari and Lotuko

The Bari and Lotuko have their own language, but they closely resemble the Dinka and are often classified along with them.

Sudanic People

The peoples who have migrated into south-west Sudan are collectively known as the Sudanic people.

During the last century the Azande moved north from Zaire into south-west Sudan. Because of their military strength and developed political organization they absorbed many of the existing inhabitants and now dominate the area. They maintain close relations with Zaire where the bulk of the Azande still live.

There are other small tribes in the south-west though most are now affiliated to the larger groups. The Bongo ('man') for example, are fairly independent and cultivate small plots of land in the wet season and hunt during the dry season. They suffered very badly at the hands of the slavers.

Many tribes in the south tattoo and scar their body for decoration and identity. Their incisors are often extracted, because it is difficult to pronounce some of the language with a full set of teeth. Most southern tribes wear an abundance of jewellery made from ivory, beads, wire or anything else they can get their hands on.

Religion

Islam is by far the main religion in the North.

According to its teachings, God revealed divine truths to Man in order to bring him back to a righteous way of life. These truths were revealed through a prophet: Adam, Noah, Abraham, Moses and Jesus were all prophets; but the greatest of all was Mohammed. Born in AD 570, Mohammed grew up to preach against the existing beliefs in his home town of Mecca. He was forced to flee from Medina, and it is this flight (**hegira**) in AD 622, that marks the first year of the Muslim calendar.

God's truths, the principles of Islam, were revealed to Mohammed by the archangel Gabriel and are documented in the Koran — the Muslim equivalent of the Bible. The five pillars of Islam are of paramount importance to the Muslims: the **shanada** or testimony that there is no God but Allah and Mohammed is his Prophet; the **haj** or pilgrimage to the kasba (the black stone in Mecca that symbolises the centre of the earth and universe) which should be undertaken by all Muslims at least once in their lifetime; the abstention from food, drink and worldly pleasures from daybreak to nightfall during **Ramadan** (the ninth month in the Islam calendar); the giving of **zakat** (alms) to the poor — usually a small percentage of one's income; the **salat** (prayers) are announced by the Muezzin five times a day — just before dawn, midday, mid-afternoon, sunset and after dark. The prayer ritual of standing, kneeling, and touching the ground with the forehead can be performed anywhere, as long as one faces Mecca; at noon on Friday, men should pray in a Mosque and listen to a sermon. Women pray at home.

The Tariqa (Pl: **Turuq**) are religious orders or fraternities based on the relationship between a shiekh, teacher or leader, and his followers. The Turuq, most colourfully known through the whirling Dervish in their patchwork gowns, are linked to Sufism — the mystical-spiritual approach to a relationship to God. Sufism is generally frowned upon by orthodox Muslims.

The **Feki** is regarded as the true Dervish with supernatural powers and renounced wordly pursuits and pleasures. He is in a position to teach the Koran and bless births and marriages.

The **Wali** is a saint who has a shrine where his followers (those who have benefitted from his **baraka** or blessing) or their descendents come and pay homage. A **zikr** (the chanting from the Koran) is sometimes held in his honour.

Mohammed Ahmed, the Mahdi, modified the five pillars of Islam and regarded himself as the representative of the Prophet. **Jihads** (holy wars) substituted the haj; **zakat** became a tax that was paid to the State; individual prayers gave way to communal prayer, and life became more puritanical.

According to tradition, the Mahdi would appear during a period of oppression—interpreted as the Turko-Egyptian rule—and after the defeat of the **Mahdiya** movement another Prophet, Isa, would emerge. During the condominium a few claimed this title, and at the time of independence some thought Abd ar-Rahman, the son of the Mahdi, would claim kingship.

The term Mahdist described followers of the movement long after the death of the Mahdi.

Religion in the South

Traditional religions are predominant in the South. In the towns, Christianity has a strong influence, and only ten per cent of the population are Muslims.

Most of the tribes believe in animism and an omnipotent God. The Dinka, for example, interpret their cosmology through cattle and believe Nhialic to be the supreme being.

The best known of the Southern religions is that of the Shilluk. They explain their existence through the legendary supreme being, Nyikang, who they claim harmonizes the Universe's three divisions: earth, sky and river.

A story goes that Nyikang was crossing the river Bahr el Ghazal when Garo, the son of the Sun, stole one of his cows. A battle ensued and Garo was defeated. Afterwards Nyikang revived his exhausted army by sprinkling them with water. This tale has an everyday allegory: the hottest time of the year immediately precedes the rainy seasons, but the Shilluk have implicit faith that every year Nyikang will defeat the Sun and bring the rains to revive the parched soil.

The traditional Shilluk concept of divine kingship is particularly famous and the main reason why they have remained such a united tribe. They believe that Nyikang is embodied in their king (reth). If the king is sick, he must die, because if he is not physically perfect then the whole tribe will suffer. Cynics say this is a good alibi for killing the king and stirring up a rebellion.

Christian missionaries arrived in the South halfway through the last century. They introduced schools and medical centres and converted many native Southerners to Christianity. There has always been friction between Islam in the North and Christianity in the South; in 1963 the government expelled missionaries from the South. Today relations are more friendly and Christianity is very evident in the South.

Ancient Sites

The ancient sites of Sudan are not so grand or well preserved as those of Egypt. However, those of Sudan are located in surroundings that are, as yet, uncluttered by tourists and souvenir sellers.

The Nile valley from the Fourth Cataract downstream and between the Fifth Cataract and the Sabaloga Gorge is rich with Sudan's ancient and Christian sites. The areas around Karima, where the Napatan kingdom flourished, and Shendi, near the ancient capital of Meroe, are especially important.

Napatan Kingdom

The actual site of the ancient city of Napata is uncertain, though it's believed to be near present-day Merowe.

Jebel Barkal (the hill which rises 100 m above the plains out-side Karima) was always regarded as sacred. After the Egyptians reconquered Sudan in the eighteenth dynasty they built their greatest temple to Amun at the foot of the Jebel (1450 BC); it remained a religious centre for the next thousand years. The great Napatan king Piankhi began rebuilding the temple in 720 BC and it was completed by Taharqa thirty years later. The sandswept remains of the 150 m long temple still exist, the altar chambers cut into the side of the hill display Pharaonic art with hieroglyphics. By the temple there is a cluster of pyramids.

Piankhi was the first of the Napatan kings to build pyramids - a custom which had long ceased in Egypt. Along with other Napatan kings, he was buried at Kurru. The pyramids average 15 m in height and 50 sq. m in base area. Many have suffered from the harsh weather conditions or from looters in ancient times. The burial chambers were cut into the ground under the pyramids.

There are eighty-two tombs at Nurri — all were once pyramids. King Taharqa was the first king to be buried here.

For details of how to get there, see p. 132.

Meriotic Kingdom

The city of Meroe was the residence of kings from the sixth century BC to the fourth century AD. Between the railway line and the river is the 120 m temple to the God Amun, originally made of brick, with its stone lions marking the site of the lion sanction. Next to it were the royal palaces and swimming pool. Water drawn by a water wheel filled the pool. One and a half kilometres to the east are the remains of the Sun temple built in 550 BC. A second building was superimposed over the temple of Isis in the first century BC and was later used by the Christ-ians. On the desert hills 5 km to the east of the ancient city are the royal pyramids; these are similar to, but in better condition than, those at Kurru and Nurri.

To get there take a train to Kabushiya, 210 km north of Khartoum; from here it's 3 km by local transport to Bagrawiya — the village by the site. The rest house is £S6 a night; £S1 if you sleep in the guard's house.

The Meriotic remains at Nagaa (40 km east of the Nile and 55 km south-west of Shendi) and Musawwaret are in better condition than the other archeological sites of Sudan. The famous Kiosk at Nagaa shows a mixture of Roman and Egyptian styles and its very characteristic of the Roman period in Egypt. On the back wall of the Lion temple the lion god is depicted with three heads and four arms, which suggests Indian influence.

At Musawwaret a large, ruined walled enclosure surrounds a temple. The purpose of the building, constructed in the first century AD, is uncertain; elephants feature in the sculpture, and it is thought they have been trained here for military purposes.

To get there take a train or bus to Shendi or Wad Ban Nagaa (40 km north-west of Nagaa) and by local transport to Nagaa. Musawwaret is between Shendi (or Wad Ban Nagaa) and Nagaa. There is a cheap hotel at Shendi but no recognized accommodation at either of the sites.

Many ancient and Christian antiquities are housed in the national museum in Khartoum, which is certainly worth a visit.

Excavations recently started in the south, but at present little is known about the region's ancient past.

The Nubian Desert between Wadi Halfa and Abu Hamed: The timetable claims the train takes thirty hours from Wadi Halfa to Khartoum. Due to stoppages it usually takes much longer. The delays provide an opportunity to get out of the crowded carriages and stretch your legs.

103

2 Information for Travellers

Visas and Permits

Visas are necessary for Sudan. The price varies according to where they are issued. In Cairo, for example, a visa costs £E10, in London three times that amount. Visas are usually valid for three months from the date of issue, but with a period of stay limited to one month. Visitors travelling overland from Egypt or Kenya are requested to wait until they reach Cairo or Nairobi respectively before obtaining a visa.

Visa regulations (and all internal permit regulations) are liable to change at short notice, so check for up-to-date inform- ation at your Sudanese Consulate or travel agent before leaving home.

If there is any indication of a visit to Israel in your passport (say, entry or exit stamps or an Egyptian visa issued in Israel with stamps mentioning Tel Aviv), you won't be granted entry into Sudan. South African nationals are also refused entry.

It's generally advisable to get all your forms (for travel within Sudan) in order in Khartoum. This not only saves time later, but an official in a provincial town may unexpectedly say he has no authority to grant you what you need.

It's worth carrying a few passport-sized photographs for visas and similar documents.

As in most Third World countries, dealing with bureaucracy is usually very time consuming. It pays to be courteous to those in authority: rules and regulations are often flexible in the hands of even the most minor official, and a pleasant approach may well bend him in your favour.

In London visas are available from the Sudan Embassy, Cleveland Row, S.W.1. Tel. 8398080

Visa Extensions

Unlike in Egypt there is no grace period once the visa has expired, though most border officials will ignore a few days over the limit. Extensions cost £S6 and are valid for two months. They are available from the Aliens' Office in Khartoum (just off the Corniche, 150 m west of the People's Palace). If you apply for an extension after being in the country only a week, make sure it is valid from when your original visa expires, not from the date of application.

Registration

You must register with the visa authorities within three days of entering Sudan. In Khartoum they are located at the Aliens' Office; in most other towns they're at the police station. If you stay in one place for more than three days, you should register with the local police.

Travel Permits

Travel permits (issued at visa offices on the spot or within twenty-four hours) are required when travelling from province to province. This is particularly important when you are in the South.

On the form you should mention all the places where you will break your journey. For example, if you are travelling from Khartoum to Wau via Nyala, enter Nyala on the form as well as Wau. This saves possible misunderstandings with local officials.

Permits are available from the visa authorities (at the Aliens' Office in Khartoum).

Obtaining Visas for Neighbouring Countries in Sudan

Visas for Kenya (£S5.20) are available only at the British Consulate in Khartoum. You need two photos and will have to wait forty-eight hours. Visas are not required by British or Commonwealth citizens (except Australians). Britons of Asian origin must register at the Consulate before going to Kenya.

A visa is valid for three months — your period of stay depends on the man who stamps your passport. At present there isn't an 'entry stamp' at Lokichokio (Kenya's first police post on the road from Sudan); ask other travellers the latest information on these formalities.

Visas for Egypt are required by everyone and again are available only in Khartoum (available from the Egyptian cultural centre in Gamhouria Avenue). The price is £S4.20 and you need two photographs. You may also be asked for a letter of approval from your embassy. It can take anything up to four days for a visa to be issued.

Visas for CAR, Chad Uganda and Zaire are available in Khartoum. The borders with Ethiopia and Libya are closed.

Re-entry Visas

Visas terminate as soon as you leave the country. If you are returning to Sudan, re-entry visas (£S10) are available from the Aliens' Office in Khartoum.

Money

The official unit of currency is the Sudanese pound (£S), which is divided into 100 piastres (PT). Money is circulated in the following demoninations:

notes: 1, 5, 10 Sudanese pounds; 25, 50 piastres

coins ½, 1, 2, 5, 10 piastres.

There are no declaration forms on entry; you can take as much foreign currency as you like into the country. However, it's illegal to take Sudanese pounds with you on leaving.

Sudan has done away with its dual rates of exchange.

The Sudanese pound is pegged to the US dollar at US$1= 90PT. The rate of exchange (Jan. '82): £S1= US$1.10; £S1 = £0.60 sterling.

In a few of the large towns it is possible to change US dollars and pounds into Sudanese pounds at 'street prices' (twenty per cent more than offered by the banks—but illegal). Avoid old torn notes as they can be difficult to pass on.

US dollars and, to a lesser extent, pounds sterling are the best currencies to take with you. Banks will not exchange Kenyan shillings or Egyptian pounds.

There are banks in most towns. Banking hours are between 8.30 am and 12 noon, Saturday to Thursday. The foreign-exchange desk at the Hilton Hotel in Khartoum is open twenty-four hours a day.

Travellers cheques are accepted by Sudanese banks. It's advisable to buy your cheques from a well known international bank, such as Barclays or American Express. For a small commission Citibank in Khartoum will cash travellers cheques for US dollars.

American Express and other major credit cards are accepted only at some top hotels and restaurants or when buying a plane ticket.

Having Money Sent Out to you in Sudan

The quickest way to receive money in Sudan is through Citibank. The sender should credit his local Citibank with the required sum, giving your full name, nationality and passport number. In turn the bank will confirm by telex with Citibank, Khartoum, that the money is ready to be collected. The whole process should take only a few days.

On the Borders

Carry a few low-denomination, hard-currency notes (say, US$1 and US$5) — you won't want to break into larger notes just before leaving the country.

Costs

If you avoid luxury and imported products which are generally more expensive than in Egypt and Europe, and eat at local cafés, sleep in Sudanese-style hotels, and travel by lorry or train, then Sudan is a cheap place to visit.

The standard meal of a vegetable dish (ful or addis with bread) costs 25PT; a bowl of boiled meat is double the price. A reasonable portion of kebabs and salad averages £S1, depending on where you eat. The ever-present cup of tea is 10PT.

Typical-Sudanese style hotels charge between £S1 and £S2 per person per night.

A train journey, for example from Khartoum to Nyala — a total of 1,320 km, travelling second-class with a fifty per cent student reduction costs £S8. The same trip by lorry sets you back £S15. Road transport fares are likely to increase rapidly as the price of petrol, which is heavily rationed, is always going up.

As an example of the prices of imports, a packet of ten Benson and Hedges cigarettes costs £S1; a small can of Carlsberg beer sells for £S1.50 in a store. Several years ago The Financial Times conducted a survey on sixty-two cities and revealed that Khartoum was the world's most expensive city in which to buy a glass of beer.

It must be remembered that costs mentioned throughout this book applied in early 1981 and are bound to increase. They should be treated as a rough guide and a comparison. Sudan's inflation rate of forty-two per cent per annum (year ending March 1980) gives an indication of the extent of the rise in prices.

Student Discounts

Students with an International Student Card are eligible to fifty per cent discount on second- and third-class rail fares. The Ministry of Youth and Sport (Wezara El Shebab) will give you a warrant to present at the station for your discount. This concession is also available on the Kosti-Juba boat. The Ministry is situated on the Corniche, about 250 m west of the People's Palace.

Post Offices

Post offices are open between 7.30 am and 1 pm and 5.30 and 6.30 p.m.

The postal system is quite reliable, but you should allow a week for mail to reach Europe — longer for the USA. International air mail stamps cost from 10 to 15PT. To send a telegram costs 25PT per word to England, 35PT to the USA.

It is cheap to send parcels abroad, though you may have to pack them in front of Customs officials.

A post restante service is provided by post offices throughout the country. Though if your name begins with M or N, or C or G, your mail may be put in the wrong pigeon hole. Some embassies receive mail for nationals.

A three-minute personal call to England costs £S15, to the USA £S20. Your call may come through in an hour — or it could take a day. If the post office is closed, try one of the big hotels. Local calls cost 5PT; most shopkeepers will let you use their phone.

Embassies

| British | PO Box 801, tel: 70760 |
| American | PO Box 623, tel: 74611 |

Sudanese Holidays

The Muslim calendar has only 354 or 355 days; consequently Muslim holidays (marked by an asterisk) fall ten to twelve days earlier each year on the Gregorian calendar. The dates are for 1982. (Muslim holiday dates are approximate.)

Independence Day	1st January
*Moulid El Nabi (the Prophet's birthday)	8th January
Unity Day	3rd March
Sham El Nassim (spring festival)	mid April (1 day)
May Revolution Day	25th May
*Eid El Fitr	21st to 24th July
*Eid El Adha (Korban Bairam)	29th September-2nd October
*Islamic New Year	18th October

Opening Hours

Shops are open from 8 am to 2 pm and 6 pm to 8 pm. Government offices are open between 8 am and 2.30 pm. Breakfast is usually taken between 9 am and 10 am.

In the North Friday is a day off; in the South it's Sunday.

Health

Vaccinations against cholera and yellow fever are recommended before entering Sudan, (check with the Sudanese Consulate before leaving home to find out whether a vaccination has been made compulsory). Get your doctor to prescribe malaria tablets before you leave home.

Take sensible precautions, for instance, disinfect and cover even the slightest cut or graze **immediately**, and wash fruit and vegetables thoroughly.

Although pharmacies supply medicines at low prices and are generally well stocked, you are advised to bring your own first-aid kit. A typical one should include an antiseptic cream or lotion; a bandage and plasters; malaria tablets; water-purifying tablets; medicine for diarrhoea and stomach upsets, and a sun-protection cream.

Hospitals and aid centres are scattered about the country — but don't expect Western standards. The private Khartoum Clinic, in the New Extension, Khartoum, is one of the better hospitals.

Tap water in the towns is usually safe to drink. However, there will be times when you have no option but to drink whatever comes your way, in these cases always add water-purifying tablets.

Be careful where you swim. Bilharzia, a disease caused by flatworms and affecting the urinary system, is contracted in slow-flowing or stagnant waters.

It should go without saying that you should be healthy and fit if you are to enjoy travelling the long distances in Sudan.

Street violence and mugging appear to be very rare in Sudan. Women are generally treated with courteous, reserved respect.

What to Wear

Take light clothing with you, although it's advisable to have a pullover for the cool winter evenings in the north, and a waterproof garment for the rainy season in the south. A hat, sunglasses, a pair of jeans and a sturdy pair of shoes are worth having if you are going to trek or ride on the back of lorries for any length of time.

Food

Sudanese cuisine is simple, bland and has little variety. The same food is eaten throughout the country (with some regional differences) by people from all backgrounds. The country occasionally suffers food shortages, although it is unlikely that you'll arrive in a village and find nothing to eat. However, if you intend to travel off the beaten track, carry a few tins of food with you.

Durra, the staple crop, is a type of maize and is often made into **kisera,** a thin unleavened bread; **gurassa** is a thicker bread. **Waker,** a sauce eaten with **kisera** or **asida** (a heavy greyish pudding) is made from **bahmiya** (okra). **Ful** (field beans) is a very popular food, particularly at breakfast; the field beans (which are similar to kidney beans) are invariably served in oil. Despite its bland taste, **ful** becomes compulsive eating. **Tamiya** is made from ground **ful** which has been fried in little balls. **Addis** are lentils. **Fasoulia** are beans to which a chunk or two of meat is sometimes added.

Sheep and goat, usually served in the form of kebabs, are the main meats eaten. Livers (**kibda**) and kidneys (**Kalawi**) are very popular.

The above dishes are served in cafes. If you eat in company, you may well use a communal bowl. There is no cutlery; instead you use your right hand and a chunk of bread.

Citrus fruits and mangoes are abundant in the right season. Limes are great thirst-quenchers. Dates, usually dried, are eaten throughout the year.

Drink

Tea (**chai**) — strong, sweet and usually without milk — is served from stalls within the country. (**Bidoon sucre** — no sugar; **Ahwayyer sucre** — little sugar; **chai bi leban** — tea with milk.)

Coffee (**kawa**) is served either in glasses or, Turkish style, in small cups. **Gibbena** is not only a type of coffee (served in small cups) but also refers to the metal container used to pour.

Kakadi is an hibiscus plant from which an extremely thirst-quenching drink is made. It both looks and tastes like blackcurrant juice.

The incessant whirring of liquidizers is becoming a common sound throughout the country; fruit juices are diluted with water.

Alcohol

In a recent wave of Islamic consciousness several provinces went 'dry'. However, compared with most Arab countries, Sudan is very tolerant of Alcohol.

Araki is a powerful alcoholic toddy made from **durra**. **Seiko,** a better-quality liquor, is made from dates (mainly found in Dongola). It is said that if you throw **seiko** into the air, it will evaporate before it reaches the ground.

Marisa, the traditional beer, is greyish in colour, heavy, and rather sour. It is sometimes served at breakfast in the villages — a nourishing way to start the day.

Duma beer, a honey beer found in the south, is light, fizzy and thirst-quenching.

Where there is no prohibition, liquor stalls sell imported spirits, wines and beers — though at exorbitant prices. Camel, the Sudanese brand of beer, is cheaper but not very good. **Watania,** Sudanese 'sherry', although comparatively cheap tastes quite unlike sherry.

Maps

Michelin and Bartholomew both publish maps of North East Africa which include Egypt and Sudan. 'Egypt' 1:3½m £3, and 'Sudan' 1:4m £2.50 have now been published in the series on the Arab World produced by Geo-Projects. The Land Survey office near the Palace in Khartoum sells detailed maps of most areas of Sudan.

Photography

Photography permits are required and are available free from the Tourist Office in Khartoum. In Juba, they are obtained from the Ministry of Information; elsewhere in the country from police stations. If you are caught taking photos without a permit, your film may be confiscated.

Sudanese, particularly in the South, are very sensitive about poverty or underdevelopment being captured on celluloid. You should, also be careful of which bridges you photograph and avoid snapping the army.

The price of film in Sudan is greater than in England; for example, Agfachrome 35 mm x 36 is as much as £S7 or £S10 with processing (at Barlaman Avenue, Khartoum). Stock and variety is limited outside Khartoum. Wait until you get home to have your photographs developed.

Newspapers

The excellent monthly English language **Sudanow** magazine (Sudan's only foreign language journal) covers current topics in Sudan. In the back is a section of useful information for visitors to the country.

Foreign newspapers are available from top hotels or relevant Cultural Centres.

Towns

Before the Egyptian invasion in the early nineteenth century there were only four large towns; all had populations of six to ten thousand and were important caravan and administrative centres. Senner, capital of the Funj kingdom, was one of the most important trading centres in Africa during the eighteenth century; Shendi was the nearest point on the Nile to Suakin; Kobbe, now non-existent, was at the start of Darb al Arbain caravan route (near present-day El Fasher); Suakin was a coastal town that dealt with imports and exports.

With the arrival of the Egyptians in 1821, towns were gradually established as administrative centres — still their main function. Today the towns, with their grid-like street plan, have no real architectural beauty and follow a standard pattern: at the centre the souk and its cafes — the pulse and charm of the town — are situated within a square of low white-washed brick buildings and, on the periphery, government houses and recent buildings. There's usually a Sudanese-style hotel, sometimes a rest house, a police station and some sort of medical aid, electricity generators, tap water, a bank, adequately stocked shops, and an open-air cinema, where English, Arabic and Indian films are shown; the atmosphere is invariably more entertaining than the film itself.

Wildlife parks

Wildlife abounds in Sudan, though unlike in East Africa it has not been exploited for the tourist industry. Neither are the game parks as picturesque, but they are certainly more pristine.

Dinder Park (6,475 sq km) is 480 km south east of Khartoum on the Ethiopian border and contains buffalo, lions, leopards, giraffes, antelope and kudu. However, at the time of writing the park is closed until further notice; normally it is open in the dry season — mid-December to late April. The tourist lodge consists of thatched bamboo bungalows with running water, electricity and a restaurant. Travel to Dinder Park is rather complicated unless you have your own transport. Trains go to Dinder station (fifteen hours from Khartoum; 80 km past Sennar on the Khartoum-Kassala line), from there it's another 175 km by road to the Galago tourist village. (Check with the Tourist Office before visiting the park).

In the South **Nimule Park** (west of Nimule) and the **Southern National Park** (between the Rumbeck and the Zande roads) do not cater for the tourist in the same way as Kenyan wildlife reserves. Big-game hunters (Sudan permits hunting) in search of lions and elephants and other animals pay vast sums for exclusive safaris. Many of the shoots take place in areas inaccessible to vehicles. Check with the safari operators in Khartoum or Juba for details of these trips.

What to buy

Many traditional handicrafts are sold in souks or by individuals. In Khartoum the tourist shops in the arcades off Gamhouria Street offer an assortment of ivory, skins, silver and wooden ornaments, as well as Sudanese objets d'art. Omdurman is well known for it's bazaar.

Transport Around the Country

Preliminary Note on Railways

The Sudan Railways Administration faces three major problems for which neither it nor the Sudanese government can be held responsible.

The first is an absence of a direct rail connection with the Egyptian system. The Egyptian government has a line running south to Aswan but seems reluctant to extend it further to Wadi Halfa. This is a vital connection not only for Sudan but also for the future of the Pan African rail network and should be tackled — quickly.

The second problem is the gauge, chosen under military duress by General Kitchener. The simple fact is that 3 ft 6 ins (Colonial or Cape Gauge) is giving way to the overwhelmingly popular Standard gauge (4 ft 8½ ins) which is already used throughout Western Europe (except in the Iberian peninsula), North America, China, and other parts of the world. In Western Asia new Standard-gauge lines are being laid, and Egypt already has them. A total, abrupt changeover would be too costly to contemplate, but the line from Wadi Halfa to Atbara should be changed to Standard gauge when the Egyptian link to Wadi Halfa is completed, and progressively onwards thereafter. In Africa, south of the equator, there is so much 3' 6" gauge track that conversion is out of the question, but north of the equator conversion must eventually come.

The third problem is the nature of the country. Sand blows across tracks and causes delays to services — an aspect that warrants total review following conversion. Building the tracks higher, sand fences, and the cultivation of special grasses are among the solutions.

The world is waiting to help Sudan establish a first-class network: not merely to aid the country itself but also because the Sudanese network forms a vital link in the projected African system.

It is becoming increasingly important for Egypt to extend its line south to the Sudan frontier as the first step in rectifying the present unsatisfactory situation. Even if Sudan had the best system in the world it would be severely handicapped without a working connection with the Mediterranean and ultimately (via western Asia and the Bosphorus) with Europe. (Contributed)

Trains

It would be most unwise to regard train timetables as part-icularly accurate: trains are prone to long and frequent delays. When asked 'What time does the train arrive?', a Sudanese will very often reply, **'Inshallah'** (It's the will of God).

When there's a backlog of freight at Pt Sudan, engines that normally pull passenger trains help to clear it. This results in a reduced passenger service — especially to the west. (At present there are only two trains a week to the west from Khartoum: one to Wau, the other to Nyala.) So long as you make arrangements with the station master beforehand, it's possible to travel in the guard's compartment on freight trains (regarded as a second class fare).

Train services link up where possible, but there are no official connections except on the rail-boat services.

Students are eligible for half-price second- and third-class rail travel (also valid for travel in the guard's compartment on freight trains).

Be sure to purchase a ticket before boarding a train: other-wise you're liable to a £S1 fine on top of the fare.

With the construction of asphalt roads, there's likely to be a swing from rail to road transport — something that's already evident on the Khartoum-Kassala route.

Classes

Trains are generally the cheapest, quickest and least uncomfort-able way to travel. They all have first-, second-, third-class and sleeper carriages.

On most trains each class has **mumtazah** ('special') carriages as well, so in effect there can be six classes plus sleepers.

Each **first-class mumtazah** compartment has six padded seats. Besides being comfortable, travel is reasonably ordered. However, the windows do not open — a great disadvantage if the air-conditioning fails. There are two sets of wide, padded bunks in each ordinary first-class compartment. In theory this is the best deal as there should only be four people to a compart-ment; in practice this number can triple.

The **second-class mumtazah** compartment, newer and in better condition than normal second-class, has six padded seats. It's worth paying a few extra pounds to travel second rather than third-class, as you're at least allocated a seat.

Third-class are through carriages with no compartments and generally very crowded. The **mumtazah** is newer and more comfortable with padded seats.

Sleeping carriages are fine, old cars with wood panelling and brass fittings. Each compartment has two bunks, with sheets, and a wash basin.

Reservations

Reservations for all first and second-class travel and sleeping compartments should be made as far in advance as possible. There are no reservations for third-class: just turn up on the day — preferably long before your scheduled departure, buy your ticket and try to find a place on the train. Carriages can become so crowded that some passengers sit on the roof.

The enquiries office at Khartoum railway station (tel: 71133/75388) is open twenty-four hours a day.

Food

There are buffet cars on most trains. Officially they are for first and second-class passengers, though there is little objection to third-class foreigners using them. The silver service and uniformed waiters provide a modest degree of elegance. Lunch and dinner (**ful**, meat, or eggs, and pudding) is fairly basic, but not bad at around £S1.50. Breakfast, at £S1, comprises an egg or **ful** dish. Tea and coffee are served most of the day. The greatest advantage of the buffet car is that it is a quiet refuge from the crowds and claustrophobia of the rest of the train.

On most routes women and children sell food and tea at the stops, but it's advisable to take some provisions and water with you.

Sample Fares

The following are approximate rail fares on Sudan Railways' main services:

Journey	sleeper	1st class	2nd class	3rd class
Wadi Halfa-Khartoum	£S34	£S18	£S12	£S4
Karima-Khartoum	£S30	£S16	£S10	£S3
Pt Sudan-Khartoum	£S30	£S15	£S 9	£S3
Khartoum-Kosti	£S15	£S 7	£S 5	£S1.50
Khartoum-Nyala	£S52	£S27	£S16	£S6
Khartoum-Wau	£S54	£S29	£S19	£S7

Fares for seats in the **mumtazah** carriages are about twenty per cent higher than those in ordinary classes.

Buses

Different companies run buses of various standards along popular routes. Try to avoid sitting at the back of the old country buses; these are battered, converted Bedford trucks — a bad bump and you are shot three feet into the air. With the construction of roads, the latest European coaches are being imported (on the Kassala-Pt Sudan highway for example); sometimes the fares are only marginally higher than on the old buses.

On most routes it is advisable to reserve your seat at least a day before departure.

River Steamers

The steamer services are described in the relevant sections of 'The Routes Through Sudan'.

Lorries

Souk (market) lorries, usually Bedford or Austin three-tonners, meticulously maintained by two young truck boys, are often the only means of getting from A to B. Passengers sit at the back on top of the merchandise. Fifteen to twenty people is good company; forty plus (which is not uncommon) — with babies, goats and hens — is distinctly a crowd and far from comfortable.

You are exposed to the elements for the entire journey: sun, sand and rain during it's season, so it's advisable to have suitable protection. What may appear to be a main road on a map is often nothing more than a lorry track. Excellent new highways are being constructed in various parts of Sudan, so the next decade should see a great improvement in road transport.

The lorries are privately owned by merchants who ferry goods around the country. The service they provide costs approximately the same as second-class rail fares — but with no student discount. Fares are sometimes fixed, sometimes negotiable; if there is a small group they usually charge less. You pay double if you sit in the cab with the driver.

Compared with a train, a lorry journey is physically more tiring and takes longer. The driver stops to sleep during the midday heat and (for a few hours) at night. As breakdowns are common, vehicles often travel in convoy: if one has a problem the rest stop and wait. I met someone who took twelve days to complete the journey between Nairobi and Juba — normally a three day trip. Most of the time was spent watching other lorries being repaired. This, I think, was an extreme case.

Once again it's worth taking something to eat with you, though there are usually opportunities to buy food along the route.

To find a lorry going your way ask around the souk or **mawgif** (lorry park).

Despite the hardships (largely compensated by the 'we're all in the same boat' camaraderie of your fellow passengers) the back of the lorry is the best and most enjoyable way of seeing the country.

Free Lifts

Hitch-hiking — in the Western sense of the word — is extremely rare except possibly on the new Khartoum-Kassala-Pt Sudan road.

There are many voluntary organizations, missionaries, construction and mining companies scattered around Sudan (in town or village, they are not difficult to locate). They have their own means of transport — landrovers, boats, planes — and are generally happy to give travellers a lift, especially in the more remote areas. I met a couple who had three free flights with a petrol company; another man hitched a lift from Juba to Malakal in a missionary boat.

Internal Flights

Sudanair operates an extensive network of internal flights. As flying is the only quick form of transport, seats are in great demand. Try and book at least a week in advance.

Here is a list of flights to some of the main towns around the country.

Route	Frequency	Price	Duration
Khartoum-Juba	daily flights, except Sunday	£S150	two hours
Khartoum-Nyala	four times a week	£S136	two hours
Khartoum-Pt Sudan	daily	£S 90	one hour
Khartoum-Wau	twice a week	£S136	two hours
Khartoum-Dongola	daily	£S 76	one hour

During the **Haj** many flights are cancelled as most of the Sudanair fleet is used to shuttle pilgrims to Mecca.

There are no discounts for foreign students.

The Effect of Weather on Travelling

Harsh physical conditions and weather, particularly during the height of the Rains (July to September in the North, May to November in the South) can have a disruptive effect on transport. The poor conditions of the roads and railways add to the difficulties.

Boat services are hardly affected by the weather, except for the Dongola-Karima steamer which doesn't operate between March and June if the Nile waters are too low. With the construction of asphalt roads and bridges the seasonal transport problems will gradually be eliminated, but for the present the traveller must have time on his hands and be prepared for delays.

Allow a couple of weeks either way for the periods of road closure given below:

North

The rainfall is not a real problem north of Khartoum, though there are some serious washouts (the washing away of the track) on the Atbara-Pt Sudan rail route. Soft sand and sand-storms can cause minor hold ups particularly during April and May.

East

With the new Khartoum to Pt Sudan highway, travelling is easy even during the Rains.

West

Trains throughout the country operate all the year round, but be prepared for delays if you are going west in July and August — especially from Barbanousa to Nyala where washouts have been known to leave passengers stranded for over a week. The rail journey south to Wau is rarely delayed more than a couple of days.

During the Rains far fewer road vehicles ply their way between Khartoum and the west, especially from Barbabousa to Nyala and Jebel Marra. You may cruise right through without any hold ups or find yourself in sight of your destination but with a powerful **wadi** (fast-flowing seasonal river) preventing you going further. It's just a matter of luck.

The Barbanousa to Wau road is closed from early May to mid November, as is the road between Nyala and CAR.

When it rains in the Nuba mountains travelling on anything but asphalt roads is difficult — sometimes impossible.

The Kadougli to Malakal road is closed from mid June to October.

South

Once the Khartoum to Kosti highway is completed the weather won't effect transport along this route.

The Kosti to Juba road is closed from May to mid November. The two roads between Wau and Juba are open throughout the year though the rains from June to November can seriously hinder travel — especially on the northern Rumbeck road. Fewer vehicles risk the journey between Juba and Kenya during the wet weather. The stretch from Torit to Kapoeta is particularly difficult — at times impassable. An asphalt road on this route — already under construction — should be completed by the mid 1980s.

Accommodation

First-Class Hotels

In Khartoum there are several internationally recognised five-star hotels and a reasonable amount of three- and four-star accommodation. Outside the capital, however, there is no accommodation of these standards; exceptions are the old colonial style hotels at Juba and Pt Sudan and the recently developed Western-style holiday resort on the coast at Arous.

Government Rest Houses

Government rest houses — usually colonial-style bungalows — are scattered throughout the country. Some are free, some require a permit, some open only to VIPs, and some charge rates ranging from 25PT to over £S12 a night. Standards are equally varied: some offer little more than a shelter, while others are comparable to three- or four-star hotels with full board.

Sudanese-Style Hotels

The typical Sudanese hotels (known as lakondas), fancily painted in sickly greens and pinks, are found in most towns around the country. They are probably the only accommodation, other than rest houses, that you'll find outside Khartoum and Pt Sudan. **Lakondas** throughout Sudan are very similar and comprise of rows of beds situated in a courtyard; small cramped bedrooms — sometimes with a fan; hole-in-the-ground lavatories, and showers — if there is running water. The conditions are basic; there is little privacy — single or double rooms are very rare. Prices range from 50PT to a couple of pounds depending on the standards.

Police Stations

The police, who are extremely helpful, will invariably put you up if you have nowhere else to stay.

Youth Hostels

There are several youth hostels around Sudan. Guests without a YHA card may have to pay an extra 10PT or 20PT.

Sleeping Out

It's advisable to carry a sleeping bag or at least a blanket as temperatures can drop dramatically at night, particularly in the desert. Unless you are keen on camping, tents are not necessary.

THE ROUTES THROUGH SUDAN

3 Aswan to Khartoum

Aswan to Wadi Halfa

The morning train takes about forty-five minutes to cover the distance from Aswan town to the Aswan harbour, from which two boats a week (on Monday and Thursday) leave for Wadi Halfa.

The harbour itself has little to offer — just a few cafés and tea stalls. Tinned food and fruit is more expensive than at Aswan. It's about a ten-minute walk to the High Dam.

The Boats

It's advisable to book your passage at least a week in advance either at the Nile Navigation Company, at Rameses Station in Cairo, or near the Tourist Office in Aswan. If you travel third-class, there's no need to book; you can buy your ticket at the Nile Navigation Company, at the harbour or on board — then it's a matter of climbing aboard and finding a space. Fares for the journey are: £E12 first-class (cabin) £E9 second-class (cabin) and £E3 third-class. All passengers are subject to a departure tax of £E1. There are no reductions for students.

There are two boats — one operated by the Sudanese, the other by the Egyptians. Both are archaic river steamers with barges strapped on either side. Only the steamer section accommodates passengers: first- and second-class cabins on the upper deck, third-class deck space down below. Conditions are basic. First-class cabins have two berths, second-class four. Third-class passengers are so crowded there's barely enough room to lie down. However, you can stretch out in comparative comfort on the flat roof over the deck.

A cook dishes up ful, soup or addis with bread for 30PT, though it's advisable to bring some food of your own. On one of the boats, a small cafeteria serves eggs, ful and kebabs. Water is pumped up from the lake and most people drink it without the (recommended) precaution of water-purifying tablets. There is always tea as an alternative.

The atmosphere of the journey to Abu Hamed is haunting — Lake Aswan in particular. Created by the High Dam, the 500 km lake (also known as Lake Nasser) has a maximum depth of around 100 m. When the lake was formed in 1963, 40,000 inhabitants (of a valley where the Ancient Nubian civilization had once flourished) had to be resettled.

The Harbour at Wadi Halfa: The former town of Wadi Halfa was submerged under Lake Aswan Dam was created in the early 1960s. Today the harbour is a jetty catering for three or four small vessels a week.

On the second night of the journey you pass **Abu Simbel**, though even if it's illuminated it's hard to distinguish its temples. Built by Rameses II between 1300 and 1233 BC it was salvaged from the valley along with other temples, tombs and antiquities before the creation of the High Dam. Unlike similar monuments it wasn't taken to a museum, but raised and placed on the edge of the present lake. UNESCO, which organized the operation, described it as the greatest archaeological rescue of all time.

The boat trip, despite its drawbacks, is by no means an ordeal; quite the contrary, it's very relaxing. You feel as if you already have one foot in Sudan.

In 1851 a Liverpool traveller named Melly arrived in Nubia from Egypt and wrote: '...We saw a good deal of the people (the Sudanese Nubians) and were much prepossessed by the simplicity and genuine integrity of their nature. After our experience of the Egyptians it was most refreshing to mingle with a race endowed with these characteristics, and living by honest industry and labour.'

Wadi Halfa

The old town of Wadi Halfa reached its height at the end of the last century with the construction of the railway by the British. It seemed a natural place to start laying the tracks: the Anglo-Egyptian army under Kitchener was coming up the Nile from Egypt in its bid to suppress the Khalifa and reconquer Sudan. Just south of Wadi Halfa was the unnavigable Second Cataract. Instead of dismantling the boats and reassembling them on the other side, it was decided to establish the railhead at Wadi Halfa. Winston Churchill, at the time a war correspondent, commented: 'A mud village was transformed into a minature Crewe.'

The old town is now under water, and most of its inhabitants have been resettled at Khashm el Girba, 65 km south west of Kassala. Today Wadi Halfa — about a kilometre from the harbour and station — is a sad cluster of houses on the desolate southern tip of the lake. The one jettied 'harbour' with a couple of tea stalls is about two kilometres from the station.

Where to Stay and Eat

Just before the station there are several rows of shops selling tinned foods.

The **Nile Hotel** (£S1) is typical Sudanese style and has a café and bakery.

There are a couple of cheaper hotels next to the shops.

Changing Money

A few dealers will approach you at the harbour. Unlike the banks they will change your surplus Egyptian pounds.

The Unity Bank (situated in the row of shops) changes travellers cheques to Sudanese pounds.

South to Khartoum

There are two routes south to Khartoum: the first direct by train via Abu Hamed and Atbara, the second by lorry along the course of the Nile through the Batn al Hagar (belly of Rocks), then via Dongola and Karima. See p. 128.

By Train from Wadi Halfa to Khartoum

The train is a connecting service for the boat and won't leave until people and goods are all on board — this can mean waiting in Wadi Halfa for the best part of the day. If the train is likely to be crowded (which is invariably the case), the station master, in an unofficial gesture of goodwill to foreigners, will sometimes tag a 'student' carriage on to the end — ordinary third-class, but at least you will have a seat. The journey to Khartoum takes about thirty hours.

It's not possible to make sleeping, first- or second-class reservations before Wadi Halfa, and there are no student reductions on the journey south.

The railway track to **Abu Hamed** , laid in 1897 by Kitchener at a rate of a half kilometre a day, cuts right across the harsh Nubian Desert — a total of 368 km. During the construction Winston Churchill wrote of the area: 'It's scarcely within the powers of words to describe the savage desolation of the regions into which the line and its constructors plunged.'

The desert is flat and stony with outcrops of barren hills — similar to those on the shores of Lake Aswan. Apart from a few desert birds and insects it's completely lifeless.

The ten stops before Abu Hamed — 'stations' no. 1 to no. 10 — consist of a handful of brick bungalows where the British built camps and bored for water during the construction of the railway. At a few of them, principally no. 6, women sell tea and sometimes food.

The ten-hour journey to Abu Hamed, on the banks of the Nile, is particularly dusty, with frequent stops to clear sand from the track. From here the railway follows the Nile to Khartoum, though the route is essentially still through desert. There are several villages along the way, and food is readily available (especially from Atbara onwards).

Get off at **Kabushiya** if you want to visit the archaeological sites at Bagrawiya; at **Shendi** or **Wad Ban Nagaa** for Nagaa and Massawerat es Suffra (see p. 101).

The journey from Abu Hamed to **Atbara** takes about ten hours; it's a further ten hours to **Khartoum**.

Abu Hamed

Abu Hamed offers the first sight of vegetation in Sudan for travellers following the train route. In the small market area by the track women sell fruit, nuts, and cakes and set up stoves to brew tea for passengers from every train — night or day.

Before the railway to Abu Hamed could be completed, the occupying Mahdist garrison had to be ousted; once this was accomplished, the town became strategically important for Anglo-Egyptian forces. The town was formerly an important stopping place for caravans crossing the desert to the Second Cataract. Today it is a railway junction with a 248 km track to Karima further to the west. The Khartoum to **Karima** train arrives at Abu Hamed early on Monday and Thursday morning; from here it takes ten hours to reach its final destination.

Abu Hamed has a couple of rows of shops and cafés and a typical colonial-style rest house (where you need permission to stay).

A ferry leaves every hour to **Mograt Island,** the largest island in the Nile basin and a former Christian stronghold.

Atbara

In 1898 three thousand Mahdists were killed by Anglo-Egyptian forces in a two-hour bloodbath at the Battle of Atbara. The town was established as a railway terminus to supply provisions to the army. It has subsequently become the headquarters of Sudan Railways.

Although it is an industrial centre, Atbara has the intimacy and character — especially around the market — of most towns around the country. The importance of the railway is certainly evident, but the town is not covered by a layer of soot, nor is there a non-stop flow of trains. The entire railway set up is both small and old enough to have charm and nostalgia.

The railway's **whasa** (workshop), with its steam engines, is interesting for train enthusiasts.

The banks of the Nile and Atbara rivers have some pleasant walks. The former British influence is still obvious in the colonial-style houses along the wide, tree-lined avenues.

The Youth and Sport centre (for student rail warrants) is in the side street next to the Watania cinema.

Where to Stay

Cross the railway line (by the track not the bridge) towards the market: The **Astoria Hotel** (£S1) is part of the shopping promenade that runs parallel to the railway track. Next to it is a drinking garden and another hotel (40PT). If you acquire a taste for the cheap Watania sherry, this is quite an amusing place to spend the evening.

On the other side of the market next to the Watania cinema is the **Atbara River Hotel** (£S1). Behind the cinema is the **Youth Hostel** (50PT) — cramped and rather dirty. Ten minutes from the station along Main Avenue is a fine colonial-style **Rest House** (£S6 for full board).

Wadi Halfa to Dongola

This stretch of the Nile has featured dramatically throughout Sudan's history — largely because of its proximity to Egypt. The Ancient Egyptian, Napatan, Christian eras and, more recently, the Anglo-Egyptian period played important roles in this area.

A couple of lorries a week (no set days) cover the route from Wadi Halfa to **Dongola.** They leave from in front of the row of shops. The fare is about £S10 and the journey takes two days. The first part of the drive, through semi desert and the Batn al Hagar, is especially tiring. You're advised to take food with you.

Distances in brackets are from Wadi Halfa.

Along the Route

There are a number of sites along the route (mainly from the Ancient Egyptian and Napatan eras), although at most of them there is little worth seeing.

Sai Island (190 km) is the site of the remains of a small temple that dates from the time of Thotmos III and a more recent Coptic church. Opposite, on the east bank, are the ruins of the Temple of Amara, built by a Sudanese queen who is buried in a tomb at Meroe.

Twenty kilometres further on is **Saddenga** and the ruins of a temple built by Amenophis III for his queen, Ti. A short distance to the south are the remains of a Coptic church.

Sulb (or Soleb) is 222 km south of Wadi Halfa. Here you can see the most significant and best-preserved Ancient Egyptian temple in the area, built by Amenophis III to commemorate his victories over local tribes.

The ruins of the temple at **Sesibi** (290 km) date from 1370 BC and are mostly underground. On the opposite bank, at Delgo, there is a rest house and a small café in the hospital. Several lorries cover the route from here to Kerma, which is 110 km further on and a good place to get a lift to Dongola in a Toyota pick-up.

Ten kilometres from Kerma is **Argo Island**, once the site of a large temple to Amun. The remains of two colossal granite statues are all that's left to see.

Kawa (435 km) is situated on the east bank, opposite Dongola. A large, Ancient Egyptian (later Napatan) town thrived here until the third century AD, when it burnt down.

On the way to the market, Dongola: Thousands of settlements cling to the Nile and owe their existence to the great river's regular flow. Dongola is one such example: its lush green orchards are irrigated by Nile waters and provide an abundant market for, amongst others, the surrounding desert dwellers.

Dongola market:

The ferry, Dongola: There are few bridges across the Nile in Sudan. Local ferries take people, animals and vehicles from one bank to the other.

Dongola

Dongola and this reach of the Nile are particularly famous for the cultivation of dates. Delightful villages and homesteads with rich, green orchards cling to the riverbanks. You don't have to travel far in north Sudan before you appreciate the beauty of such lushness.

The picturesque market behind the main square stocks an abundance of fruit and vegetables. There is a rest house, and a couple of cheap hotels near the hospital. Old Dongola, with its Christian remains, is 125 km upstream.

Moving On

The steamer to **Karima** leaves on Sundays (sometimes there's one mid week as well). The vessel is of a similar standard to the one plying the route between Aswan and Wadi Halfa and with the same classes — but no barges. Third-class (deck) travel costs £S4; the journey is pleasant and relaxing and takes three days. (The steamer does not operate from March to June, when the Nile waters are low.)

There are two lorry routes south: either along the Nile via Ed Debba and Korti to **Merowe** (price: £S7; duration: one day), or directly across the desert (£S6; twelve hours). The second route is more popular with merchants because it is shorter; however, you travel across flat, stony desert on a road that is little more than tracks made by the previous lorry. (The duration of the trip depends largely on the skill of the driver in avoiding the soft sand).

Two buses leave on Saturday and another two on Tuesday bound for **Khartoum** via Ed Debba. The Nimeiri Express, a new, non-stop, first-class bus takes twelve hours (fare: £S18); The ordinary country bus takes a day and a half and costs £S8. Lorries also cover the journey on most days.

Karima and Merowe

The sandswept towns of Karima and Merowe on the banks of the Nile are in the location of some of Sudan's most historic sites. (see 'Ancient sites' P. 100). Twenty kilometres downstream from Karima is the royal Napatan cemetery of Kurru, while Jebel Barkal, with its temple of the God Amun, is 2 km out of town.

Karima is an important rail and steamer terminus. There is a cheap hotel between the station and the hospital. Ferries cross

Between Karima and Dongola, the desert route:: If there are no roads or tracks, then drivers rely on the sun or stars to guide them to their destination. Souk (market) lorries travel throughout Sudan and are a recognized means of transport for goods and passengers.

133

Jebel Barkal, Karima: The windswept area around Jebel Barkal is where the Napatan civilization prospered from about 720 BC. An appeal of the ancient sites in Sudan is that they lie in their natural surroundings undeveloped for tourism. The reasons are because the sites are, first, fairly inaccessible- second compared to Egypt the sites are not very spectacular and third, tourism in ʿsudan has been rather slower to develop.

the river regularly to Merowe and the lush village of Nurri. There is little to see of historical importance at Merowe, though it is claimed to be the site of the ancient city of Napata. The pyramids at Nurri are 10 km upstream and 2 km inland.

Moving On

Lorries and buses leave for **Khartoum** several times a week from both Karima and Merowe via the direct route through the Baiyuda Desert. The fare is £S6, and the journey takes one day.

Trains leave at 12.30 pm on Wednesdays and Sundays. The journey from Karima to **Abu Hamed** takes twelve hours, from Abu Hamed to Khartoum, twenty hours. Rail is the only means of transport to Abu Hamed. The train passes through desert and touches the banks of the Nile only once.

Pyramids, Jebel Barkal: Today most of Sudan's ancient temples and Pyramids are in ruins having suffered under the harsh environment and at the hands of grave robbers.

4　The Port Sudan Loop

Atbara to Port Sudan

In 1906 the Red Sea Hills railway to Pt Sudan was completed, thus linking Khartoum with the coast. This had a tremendous effect on the country's economy; exports more than doubled in two years. The only way from Atbara to Pt Sudan is by rail — conditions are too severe for most road vehicles. It's another dusty scrub-desert train ride with the usual stops and taking around eighteen hours to cover the 474 km route.

If you want to miss out Pt Sudan, you can get off at **Haiya Junction** and catch a bus to **Kassala;** the tarmac road is an excellent route and quicker than the train (which comes via the junction from Pt Sudan to Kassala once a week). The problem is that buses usually start their trip full, so there may not be room to pick up anyone on the road.

The Khartoum to Pt Sudan train passes through Atbara early on Wednesday and Friday mornings.

Port Sudan

At the beginning of the century it became apparent that Suakin was too small to cope with the large ocean steamers. Mersa-Sheikh Barghut (named after Sheikh Barghut, a holy man whose body is said to have floated from Arabia) was chosen as the site of the new port. It was renamed Port Sudan and officially opened by the Khedive of Egypt in 1906.

As a new industrial town without an indigenous population, Port Sudan attracted different ethnic groups eager to make money. Merchants came to set up shop and a lot of money changed hands at all levels as industry and trade developed. Today, Port Sudan is a more blatant cosmopolitan commercial centre than anywhere else in the country.

It's an interesting place to visit, though most foreigners find it dirty and more expensive than elsewhere in the country. The real attractions for tourists are the coral reefs.

Registration is at the Governor's Office in the large white building between Olympia Park and the waterfront. The Commissioner here will give you written permission to stay at the rest house at Suakin.

Student rail discounts are available from the Youth and Sports Centre in the Transit area, five-minute's ride from the town's main bus area.

The **tourist office** is next to the Red Sea Hotel.

Diving

The Red Sea off Sudan is reputed to have some of the most beautiful coral reefs in the world. Diving tours come to Pt Sudan and spend a fortnight at a time out at sea. These are expensive. For the individual traveller it's worth going to the yacht harbour (facing the sea from the waterfront, follow the promenade to your right), where there are usually one or two yachts running day trips to the reefs. These charge around £S25, which includes tanks, snorkeling equipment and lunch. If you are at all interested in marine life, that's cheap. You could also try the fishermen further round the harbour.

The **Red Sea Club** halfway along the waterfront is an expatriate's haven where there is always someone to give you information on the best — and worst — places to dive, who's taking boats out, where to avoid sharks, and so on.

The **Marine Office** — more or less opposite the Red Sea Club — sends a boat twice a month to **Zangareb Lighthouse,** site of one of the most beautiful coral reefs. The trip, about two hours each way, is free. Glass-bottomed boats also leave from here and chug around just outside the harbour.

Hamido Tours in the town centre operate excursions out to sea.

Deim Arabi

Deim Arabi is a shanty area, with a sprawling market. It's not particularly attractive, but it is almost exclusively Hadden-dowah. If you look around, you'll find handicrafts at prices that are cheaper than most other places. (From the main bus area in town, Deim Arabi is a five-minute ride directly inland). The rows of cheap cafes in another nearby shanty area around Deim Suakin are packed with people in the evening.

Where to Stay

There is a shortage of accommodation in Pt Sudan — especially during the Haj when pilgrims stop on their way to Mecca. Rooms are crowded, and the humid climate and mosquitoes only make the situation worse.

If you face the police station from the main bus area, most of the hotels are located down the third and fourth streets to your right. One of the cleaner cheap hotels is the **Khartoum Pension** (£S1.50 per head a night). However, you have to find a bed where you can; if needs be the police will take care of you.

Towards the harbour, next to the Governor's Office, is the **Red Sea Hotel,** which still retains much of its colonial style. A couple of blocks to the right is the new **Palace Hotel.** Both, at £S40 per person a night, are the best hotels in town.

In the middle price range, the **Olympia Hotel** overlooks the park opposite the statue of Osman Digna, Prices start from around £S18 per head per night.

Where to Eat

Besides the usual cafes around the souk, and the main hotels, there is an outdoor cafe in the middle of Olympia Park; this serves kebabs, ful and omelettes and is open until quite late at night. Behind the Khartoum Pension there is a good ful and beans courtyard. Fresh water is pumped to Pt Sudan from several kilometres away and can cause minor stomach upsets.

Moving On

Microbuses (minibuses) and Boxes (see glossary) leave for **Suakin** from Deim Suakin, the fare 60PT, and the journey takes forty-five minutes.

A first-class bus which leaves Deim Suakin for **Kassala** every day (7 am - £S6) takes ten hours on the new tarmac road. There is also one train a week.

The road between Pt Sudan and Atbara is more or less disused now; the train is the only means of transport. If you travel from Pt Sudan to **Khartoum** by bus, you have to change at Kassala.

The railway station is a ten-minute walk from the town centre. The train leaves Pt Sudan at 1 pm on Saturday. It's an eighteen-hour journey to **Atbara** and another ten hours to Khartoum.

The reality of the romantic dream of catching a boat to the East — or even just up and down the coast for that matter — is a weary trudge around the harbour and straight refusals from boat-owners. Very occasionally you can work for your passage; if you know something about sailing, try the yacht harbour — but don't be too optimistic. There is a ferry to Jeddah, Saudi Arabia.

Kitchener's headquarters, Suakin: Kitchener occupied this small fortress at the end of the last century, when he was in charge of a garrison of Anglo-Egyptian forces stationed in Suakin. One room now houses the gun and various garments belonging to Osman Digna, the Mahdist national hero. With permission it is possible to stay here.

Arous

The model, Western-style beach resort 40 km north of Pt Sudan, provides bungalow accommodation at £S40 a night, water skiing, snorkelling and so on. Bookings are made through the Red Sea Hotel.

Erkowit

This is a beautiful hill retreat, 40 km south-west of Pt Sudan, frequented by the rich and by honeymooning couples. It's difficult to reach unless you have your own transport. Arrangements for staying at the old hotel — empty most of the year — should be made through the Red Sea Hotel. Alternatively you can camp. (See the Tourist Office for information on transport).

Suakin

Suakin is unique. About sixty years ago H.C. Jackson wrote: 'Suakin is a magic little town, a city of Arabian Nights, fantastic, aloof... few can fail to be affected by the restful mystic charm.' He went on to say that the houses were beginning to fall down because trade had dwindled and everyone was leaving for the newly created Pt Sudan. Today Suakin Island is almost completely deserted. The one time five-storeyed houses — built from white coral and in the same architectural style as Jeddah — are in ruins. The decay is solely due to weathering and lack of maintenance.

A story tells how Suakin got it's name. The King of Abyssinia gave a present of seven beautiful virgins to the King of Egypt. A eunuch was sent ot collect them, and on his return journey spent the night with them on an island. On their arrival in Egypt, it was discovered that the 'virgins' were pregnant. The girls claimed that while on the island they had been visited by a **jinn** (spirit) and that he was the cause of their misfortune. To account for their pregnant state, they said **'Sawwa Jinn** ('the jinn did it) — hence the name Suakin. The girls were sent back to the island, and it is from them that the former inhabitants of Suakin are supposedly descended.

The history of Suakin goes back over a thousand years, though it wasn't until 1428 that it became the major port in the western Red Sea after the sacking of Aidhab — the other large port on the coast. Caravans of up to a thousand camels would bring copper, ivory, hides and slaves from the interior and return with cotton, spices, silks and beads. By the sixteenth century the harbour could accommodate two hundred ships and galleys.

The stairway in the main courtyard, Kitchener's headquarters, Suakin.

142

A boxed window in the main courtyard, Kitchener's headquarters, Suakin.

With the Egyptian colonisation in the nineteenth century, Suakin became even more cosmopolitan and was the only town in Sudan not to fall to the Mahdists during their rule at the end of the last century. With the building of Pt Sudan, Suakin's importance declined, but even up to the 1950's, 20,000 pilgrims would leave from here to Jeddah each season. Today it's cheaper to fly.

The present town, **El Geif**, is on the mainland, connected to the island by a 100 m causeway. It's rather run down and, with its swarms of flies and lack of fresh water, there is an unhealthy air about the place.

Fishermen bring in a variety of fish (barracuda eyes are a delicacy) which they sell at the harbour. There are a few cafés and an early-morning market. The shops are not well stocked with anything of any use; what tinned food they have is expensive.

It's safe to swim off the island, or fishermen will happily take you to the reefs — the best ones are a couple of hours along the coast.

The best known building in Suakin — just before the causeway — is the deteriorating caravanserai built by the merchant Shennawi Bey in 1881. It had 354 rooms — one for each day of the year (according to the lunar calendar).

Where to Stay

The **Rest House**, Kitchener's old headquarters, is a mini fort and still retains a distinct colonial atmosphere. It overlooks the harbour — if you lean over the verandah the incredibly clear water is directly below. The building is empty and slowly falling into disrepair. Few people stay here: your sole companions will probably be the pigeons in the eaves and, supposedly, Kitchener's ghost. There is no electricity or water.

You need permission from the Commissioner at the Governor's Office in Pt Sudan before staying here. The caretaker lives somewhere on the island.

There is no other recognised accommodation. Villagers may put you up, or you can camp.

Moving On

It's difficult to get to **Kassala** — unless you try hitching — without first going to Pt Sudan. There are 'boxes' leaving all the time for **Pt Sudan** (fare: 60PT, duration: 45 minutes).

The jebels (hills) at Kassala: Many folktales are attached to the bare jebels of Kassala. The climber of the Toteel peak is bestowed with special powers and longevity; apparently this summit has yet to be conquered.

145

The souk (market), Kassala: For most of the year Kassala gets its water from an underground supply. This also irrigates the rich orchards which provide the town with a large and plentiful market.

Kassala

Kassala is one of the jewels of Sudan. Its main attraction is the bizarre sugar-loaf **jebels** (hills) which sprout out of the ground and, from a distance, look like a top-heavy cloud formation. The smooth, slightly curved surface of the granite is a result of exfoliation — a type of desert erosion. The smaller of the two jebels, Toteel, has apparently never been climbed. At the summit of Taka (930 m), on the right as you look from Kassala, is the Tree of Eternity, whose leaves have magical powers. Taka is said to be one of the best rock climbs in Africa — though only for the experienced climber.

The town's large, compact and extremely varied market is certainly one of the best in Sudan. What makes it even more colourful is the hotch-potch of different cultures. The Beja with their decorative combs in their hair; the flamboyant Eritreans — mostly refugees; the prosperous Indian merchants, doing roaring trade with their imported 'cotton' (invariably nylon or polyester); the short turbanned Raishada men, who look like something out of the Arabian Nights, and their fiery-eyed, heavily veiled women, who almost maul you in an attempt to sell their jewellery.

There is the usual old colonial section of town presided over by the local administrators. Kassala was one of the last outposts of Egyptian resistance before it finally fell to the Mahdists in 1885. The town was captured by the Italians — who were based in Ethiopia — in 1894, and three years later handed over to the Anglo-Egyptian forces.

Where to Stay

There are quite a few cheap hotels: the best value for money is the **Africa** in the souk area: £S1 a night, or only £S1.50 each for a double room.

Up the road from here, away from the market, is the best hotel in town, the **Toteel** (£S6 for a single).

Near the Shell station, on the corner of the Main Avenue, are the typically Sudanese-style **Taka** and **Watania** hotels (£S1 a night). There are plans to reopen the youth hostel at the Casino (or gardens) just outside town on the Khartoum Road.

Where to Eat

One traveller with a wildly romantic imagination described Kassala as the Paris of Sudan; the similarity being the locals' attitude towards café life. As well as the many cafés in the market, there is the **Ashana** ('our supper') along the main avenue away from the town centre and a couple of blocks past the Shell station. It serves only meat dishes — kidneys, liver, kebabs — but is probably the best eating place in town.

Khatmiya

Khatmiya is at the base of the jebels. The slightly decaying mosque of Sayed El-Hassan, the highly revered paternal figure of Kassala, is just outside the village. His father founded what turned out to be the Khatmiya religo-political fraternity which gives the village its name.

Regular buses leave Khatmiya from opposite the vegetable market. It's a twenty-minute trip.

Moving On

There are at least three buses leaving for **Khartoum** each morning from different parts of town. At the time of writing the most comfortable was the New Express, leaving from outside the Africa Hotel. All companies charge around £S6. The twelve-hour trip is through flat, rather drab country.

Buses for **Gedaref** leave daily. The four-hour journey costs £S3.

The very comfortable Abu Khalil bus leaves for **Pt Sudan** every morning from a spot a couple of roads down from the Watania Hotel. The trip takes ten hours and costs £S6.

Gedaref

This is the centre of one of the richest agricultural areas in Sudan. The town, with its large Ethiopian refugee population, is not ot particular interest to the tourist.

5 Khartoum

Khartoum, at the confluence of the Blue and White Niles, is known as the Tri-Town capital, comprising of Omdurman, Khartoum and Khartoum North. In Arabic the name means 'elephant's trunk', due to the shape of the land between the rivers just before they meet.

In 1821, during Egypt's colonisation of Sudan, Ismail established a military post at Khartoum — at the time only a small village. Its strategic position resulted in its gradual growth, and in 1834 the capital was transferred from Sennar (280 km south-east). During the next fifty years European explorers, government envoys, missionaries, scientists and traders (particularly in ivory and slaves) based themselves in Khartoum.

Many were corrupt and dishonest. The Nile explorer, Samuel Baker, remarked: 'As the water of a river deposits it's impurities upon meeting the salt waters of the sea, so we find the dregs of the human race at these points where savage receives the pollution of semi-civilization.'

The immorality was matched by sickness: cholera and typhus epidemics in the mid 1850s and early 1860s led Baker further on his path of condemnation: 'A more miserable and unhealthy spot than Khartoum can hardly be imagined.'

The rise of the Mahdi, the siege of Khartoum and its subsequent fall (with the death of General Gordon in January 1885) ended an era. Khartoum was ransacked, and the Madhi moved the capital to Omdurman — until then only a camp for his soldiers. Under the Khalifa, Omdurman, built in Islamic fashion in concentric circles round a mosque, became the heart of the Mahdist state and grew rapidly as the Khalifa brought supporters here from all over the country.

At the end of August 1898 Kitchener, heading an Anglo-Egyptian force, arrived by river at Khartoum with the intention of avenging Gordon's death. On 2nd September, 11,000 of the Khalifa's army were killed at the Battle of Omdurman; the Anglo-Egyptian forces lost only forty-nine men. The victorious Kitchener rebuilt Khartoum as the capital. The street plan was designed to follow the lines of the Union Jack — it was thought that such a layout would make the defence of the city easier.

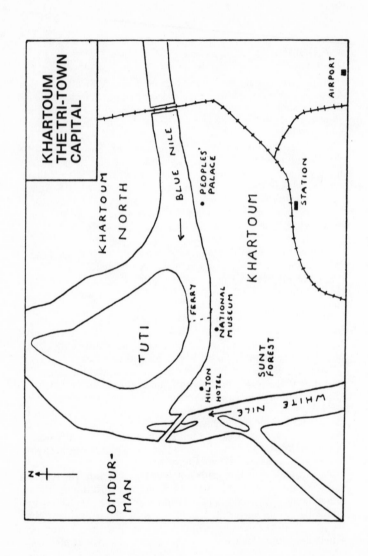

KHARTOUM
THE TRI-TOWN
CAPITAL

KHARTOUM NORTH

BLUE NILE

PEOPLES' PALACE

FERRY

NATIONAL MUSEUM

HILTON HOTEL

TUTI

KHARTOUM

SUNT FOREST

WHITE NILE

STATION

AIRPORT

OMDUR-MAN

N

Named after Om Durman (the woman in the sun), sprawling Omdurman has been little affected by modern development and retains its Mahdiya character: mud-brick buildings and narrow bustling alleys. It's an example of traditional Sudanese urban life.

At the beginning of the century, Khartoum North was established as the industrial area, a role it still maintains.

Khartoum Today

Khartoum is certainly Sudan's sophisticated, international centre. In common with other Third World capitals, Western-style affluence, with its Mercedes and expensive hotels, is juxtaposed with the traditional way of life. But the contrasts, unlike those of other developing cities, are by no means horrifying. There is no teeming urban poverty in squalid, overcrowded shanty towns; nor are there multimillion-pound, 25-storey skyscrapers along the rather stunted Khartoum skyline. Maybe this will change. Sudan is certainly developing: multinational companies, foreign businessmen and inter-national-aid programmes are increasingly evident. But as an international capital Khartoum, with it's pleasant tree-lined avenues and it's Corniche, is still peaceful and small with an easy-going atmosphere.

Where to stay

Khartoum has a reasonable range of hotels with prices from 50PT to £S70 per head per night. All those mentioned, except the Youth Hostel, Green Village and the Friendship Palace, are within walking distance of the town centre.

Inexpensive

At 50PT a night the **Student House** is the cheapest place in town. Most rooms contain two or three bunks. The front door is closed at 11 pm, but it's usually possible to get in later. You can camp in the garden.

The Student House and the **Royal** are the most popular hotels with travellers. At the Royal, people sleep four or five to a room; there are also beds in the courtyard. The general setting and atmosphere is pleasant, with a restaurant and bar in the garden. A bed for the night costs £S1.

The **Roxy** is next to the Royal. It is a similar establishment, though more spacious and with fewer travellers (£1.80 per person per night).

The **Youth Hostel** has recently opened in Street 29 of the New Extension. There is an 11 pm curfew. The hostel charges £S1 per person per night.

If you continue along Sayed Abdul Rahman Avenue, you'll come across many cheap hotels on the other side of Quasr Avenue. Most are crowded and not very clean. Three of the better ones are: **Arkweit,** a typical small, cheap hotel (£S1 per person per night); **El Nahrain,** which is comparatively clean and spacious (£S1.50 per person per night or from £S4 for a double room); and **Bahral Al Ghazal,** a rather gloomy establishment situated in Souk Arabi with four beds to a room (90PT per person per night).

Pension Nilein, in Abu Sinn Street, is small, quiet and clean with a pleasant garden (£S2.50 per person per night, or £S5 for a double room).

The **Lido** and the **Asia** are well known, relatively inexpensive (around £S3.50) hotels just off UN Square. Both are somewhat dark and drab. A double room with bath at the Lido is £S8. is £S8.

There are several hotels in Omdurman. The **Abir,** near the post office (£S1 per person per nights) is the most convenient place to stay if you have early-morning transport to catch from Omdurman.

Moderate

The **Safa** charges £S17 for a double room (£S10 for a single), which includes bath, air-conditioning and breakfast. Conditions are basic but the hotel is clean. The **Swahili** is fairly similar, although cheaper and with no private bathrooms.

El Shark offers the best value in this price bracket. It has a garden, restaurant, and bar and is less claustrophobic than similar establishments. A single room with bath and air cooler costs £S8.50.

If you have a British or Commonwealth passport, you can get a room at the **Sudan Club** (from £S15) and have full use of their facilities (swimming pool, squash courts, etc.).

Expensive

The following hotels are all of three- or four-star standard. All rooms have private bathrooms and air-conditioning.

The **Oasis** is small and quiet with a garden and swimming pool. A single room costs £S25, double £S42.

The **Excelsior** is under the same management as the Oasis and is very similar in standard and rates, although it's larger and with a less personal atmosphere.

The **Sudan** is a fairly dour hotel, situated on the Corniche. Rates are £S35 for a single, £S55 a double room.

The **Meridien** is part of an international French hotel chain. It's new, large and with every amenity, including a swimming pool. A single room costs £S40, £S48 a double.

The **Arak** is the other high-rise building that dominates the Khartoum skyline. It's of a similar standard and price to the Meridien, but without a swimming pool.

Green Village is a small bungalow complex, with tennis courts, pool and other facilities. It's situated on the banks of the Blue Nile at Burri. Prices start from £S38 for a single room.

The three five-star hotels — The **Grand, Hilton** (both along the Corniche), and the **Friendship Palace** — have the facilities of any top hotel. The prices are around £S65 for a single and £S75 for a double room (the Grand is not quite as expensive).

Of the three, the Friendship is the best; however it's sadly neglected as it's located in Khartoum North — away from the city centre.

Where to eat

There are cafes all over Khartoum, though they are mainly concentrated around UN Square and Souk Arabi (a few of the better ones are marked on the map). Some of the cheaper hotels serve Sudanese dishes in the evening. Nearly all the middle range and top hotels and clubs have Western food of various standards.

Kasa Blanka and Bimbos are Western ice-cream parlours, with milkshakes, beefburgers and chips also on the menu. The Railway Cafe at the station is a slightly upmarket variation on the same theme, specializing in kebabs.

'Eat-as-much-as-you-like' buffets are certainly good value once in a while and especially welcoming if you have been travelling around the country.

The American Club and the Sudan Club hold their buffets at Friday lunchtime. The price is £S2 a head.

The Meridien 'eat as much as you like' meals: continental breakfast for £S2.50; American breakfast for £S4.50, and lunch and dinner for £S9. The Hilton, which also offers an English breakfast, charges slightly more for the same type of deal.

Al Boustan One (for Chinese food) and Al Boustan Two (a general Western menu) are regarded as two of Khartoum's best eating places. An average three-course meal costs around £S8. Both restaurants are in Khartoum Two district — an half-hour walk south from the town centre.

Where to go for more information

The Tourist Office in Hurriya Street are happy to give help and information on all aspects of both Khartoum and Sudan in general. The Ministry of Culture and Information (Gamaa Avenue) is another source of useful information.

At the back of the magazine, **Sudanow,** is a section entitled 'What's On in Khartoum'; this contains ideas of what to see and where to go.

The Aliens Office, just off the Corniche, looks after registration, the issue of travel permits and visa extensions.

What to do

The large bustling **Omdurman souk,** with its famous gold street (near the taxi terminus) is best visited in the early evening. Its selection of handicrafts is rather overrated. Boxes leave from opposite Farouk Mosque in Khartoum; the 8 km journey takes ten minutes.

The Camel Market (Souk Gamel), in Omdurman, is situated by the microwave mast, approximately two kilometres north of Omdurman's main souk and consists of a handful of herdsmen and dealers with camels scattered around a large dusty expanse on the edge of town. If you are travelling around the country — especially in Kordofan — you should come across more colourful camel markets. The camel market is open daily.

Hamed El Nil's body was washed up, in perfect condition, seventy-five days after his death. He was proclaimed a saint and brought to Omdurman. Every Friday members of his Tariqa (religious order) come to his Mosque in the drab graveyard on the outskirts of Omdurman and perform the zikra (religious chanting) and **Dervish Dancing.** A circle of several hundred people form the arena. The Dervish, many in patchwork jibbah gowns, and anyone caught up by the fervour of the ritual, dance, whirl, fall into convulsions and do anything they want as the background of chanting, rhythmic beating of drums and clashing of cymbals gradually reaches a frenzied crescendo. Everyone is welcome. Dervish dancing takes place on Friday afternoon from 3.30 until sunset. You can catch a box from opposite Farouq Mosque going on the Banat Route to Omdurman. Get off at Banat, from where its a fifteen minute walk or a box ride to the graveyard (ask anyone the way).

Near the Hamed El Nil Mosque there's **wrestling** — Sudanese style — every Friday starting around 4 p.m. It attracts large crowds and is quite amusing.

The dervish in his patchwork or green 'jibbah' appears to be in a total trance as he whirls to the rhythmic beating of the drums.

The Mahdi's tomb, Omdurman: The Mahdi led the successful nationalist uprising against the Egyptians which culminated in 1885 with the assassination of General Gordon, who had been sent to Khartoum by the British government to evacuate the Egyptian troops.

Abdullahi Khalifa succeeded the Mahdi and developed Omdurman during his years in power. **Khalifa's House,** his mud-brick dwelling, houses a simply and extremely effectively laid-out museum containing sepia-photos and relics of the Mahdi-Gordon, Khalifa-Kitchener era. At the entrance to the museum is the boat used by Jean Baptiste Marchand in his mission to Fashoda. Khalifa's House is open from 8.30 am to 8.30 pm, Tuesday to Sunday; 8.30 am to 12 noon and 3.30 pm to 8.30 pm, Friday; closed Monday. Entrance: 10PT. To get to the museum, take a box travelling along the Murada Route to Omdurman from opposite Farouq Mosque to the Beit El Khalifa.

Mahdi's Tomb, with its dazzling silver dome, is next to the Khalifa's house. In 1898 the original mosque was destroyed by Kitchener, who ordered the Mahdi's bones to be thrown into the Nile. The tomb was rebuilt in its present form in 1947 by the Mahdi's son. Foreigners are not allowed to enter.

Tuti Island, at the confluence of the Blue and White Niles, is now an important market garden for Khartoum. Its inhabitants are Mahas from north Sudan who settled here before the Funj Sultanate of Sennar. A ferry leaves for Tuti every fifteen minutes from outside the Friendship Hall.

The collection of the **National Museum** mainly consists of antiquities from Sudanese Nubia, including the Temples of Buhin and Semna West (1500 BC), brought here when Lake Aswan was formed. There is also a selection of Christian art and artefacts that date from the seventh to the eleventh century. The museum, situated on the Corniche, is well laid out. It is open from 8.30 am to 8.30 pm, Tuesday to Sunday; 8.30 am to 12 noon and 3.30 pm to 8.30 pm, Friday. Entrance: 10PT.

With Sudan's ethnographic potential, it's a pity that the **Ethnographic Museum** is not larger. The displays are eclectic and information scant, but it's certainly worth a visit as most of the artefacts on show are still used by tribes around the country. The museum is situated on Gamaa Avenue and is open from 8.30 am to 1.30 pm, Saturday to Thursday; 8.30 am to 12.30 pm, Friday; closed Monday. Entrance: 10PT.

The **Natural History Museum** houses an impressive collection of stuffed birds. Models of Sudanese fauna are displayed in replicas of their natural habitat, A reptilery contains tortoises, crocodiles and snakes. It is located on the Gamaa Avenue and is open from 8.30 am to 1.30 pm, Saturday to Thursday; 8.30 am to 12.30 pm, Friday; closed Monday. Entrance: 10PT.

The **Zoo**, on the Corniche, has deteriorated in the past few years as there are plans to build an elaborate animal complex on the banks of the White Nile, in the Sunt Forest.

Mograin Family Gardens is a funfair situated between the Hilton Hotel and Omdurman Bridge. There is an entrance fee.

Situated on the banks of the White Nile behind the Hilton Hotel, the **Sunt Forest** is a popular Friday picnic ground and a campsite for overland expeditions. Another popular picnic spot is **Jebel Aulia,** a reservoir 53km south of Khartoum.

If you stand on the **Khartoum North Bridge** between the months of November and May and look towards the confluence of the White and Blue Niles, you can distinctly see where the creamy waters of one river and the blue waters of the other meet without actually mixing. They continue side by side until the Sabaloga Gorge, 65km downstream.

Cultural Centres are libraries (the British Council has quite a good selection of books on Sudan) for foreign communities. They have fairly up-to-date newspapers and magazines, and also show films and stage plays. Anyone is welcome. Most of the centres keep normal business hours.

Horse racing in Khartoum is not of a particularly high standard. Camel races are sometimes held but it's difficult to find out when. In either case, betting is permitted. The racecourse is near Souk Shaby (5 km south of the town centre). Races begin at 2.30 pm Friday and Saturday. Entrance: 50PT.

The Tourist Office organizes a two-hour **boat trip** along two Niles around Khartoum. However, it only operates when there are enough passengers. All bookings have to be made at the Tourist Office. Price: £S1 a head.

One of the Meridien Hotel's excursions is the **'Nile Trip'**, again in the Khartoum vicinity but with lunch and soft drinks included in the price of £S10 a head.

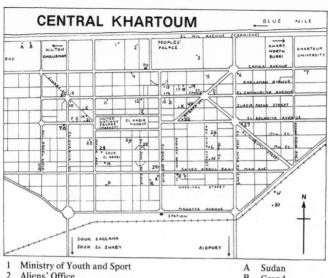

CENTRAL KHARTOUM

1   Ministry of Youth and Sport
2   Aliens' Office
3   Land Survey Department
4   Ministry of Culture and Information
5   British Council
6   Ethnographic Museum
7   Natural History Museum
8   Boxes: to Omdurman
9   Farouq Mosque
10 Gordon Music Hall
11 Egyptian Cultural Centre (visa applications)
12 24 hour Pharmacy
13 British Embassy
14 Athenae - recommended, cheap restaurant
15 American Embassy
17 Kasa Blanka Cafe
18 Bimbos Cafe
19 Sudan Club
20 Recommended, cheap restaurant (no name)
21 Alekhlas - recommended, cheap restaurant
22 Boxes: to Khartoum North and Burri
23 Atlas - recommended, cheap restaurant
24 Zibadi - recommended, cheap restaurant
25 Boxes: to Airport and New Extension
26 British Consulate
27 Citibank
28 Boxes: to Souk Saggana and Souk El Shaby
29 American Centre
30 American Club

A   Sudan
B   Grand
C   El Shark
D   Excelsior
E   Swahili
F   Safa
G   Asia
H   Lido
J   Arak
K   Acropole
L   Pension Nilein
M   Bahral El Ghazal
N   Oasis
P   El Nahrain
Q   Arkweit
R   Meridien
S   Roxy
T   Royal
W   Student House

P.O. Post Office
T.O. Tourist Office

* Peoples' Palace: The President's Palace and the site where
  General Gordon's Palace once stood.

159

The best and most accessible place to **swim** in the Blue Nile is by the Green Village Hotel at Burri; there are other beaches slightly further up the river. It's not safe to swim in the White Nile at Khartoum, because of both the current and the risk of contracting bilharzia.

The Blue Nile, Coliseum (open air) and the Friendship Hall **cinemas** are all in the centre of Khartoum. Films shown are either in English (often recent box-office hits), Arabic, Indian or French.

The Hilton and Meridien hotels show video films daily, but admission is limited to residents and their guests. There are also regular film shows at the Cultural Centres.

Gordon's Music Hall, Khartoum's only well established **night club**, has Western-style floor shows featuring European show girls.

The Meridien, Friendship Palace, Excelsior and Green Village are among the big hotels that have **discos**.

Much of Khartoum's socializing takes place in a number of clubs. The two main ones, the **American Club** and the **Sudan Club** (patronised by the British) are situated in the middle of town and offer the best facilities. A member has to sign you in and for £S1 a day at the American Club or £S2 a day at the Sudan Club, you can make use of the pool, restaurant and other amenities.

How to get about

Most places of interest in Khartoum are within reasonable walking distance of each other. To go slightly further afield, **'Boxes'** (Toyota pickups converted into large-scale taxis) are the best bet; fares rarely exceed about 10PT. They follow particular routes, and although it's theoretically possible to flag them down in the street they're usually full. Buses are marginally cheaper but are also very crowded; micro-buses have been introduced on some routes.

Main routes are:

to **Souk Saggana** 3 km and **Souk El Shaby** 5 km: box from Souk Arabi; to **Omdurman**: box from opposite Farouq Mosque, or bus from El Kabir Mosque; to the **airport** and the **New Extension** (**Amarat**): box from El Jami Avenue (between El Quasr Avenue and Souk Arabi); **to Khartoum North and Burri:** box from Baladiya Avenue by the Credit and Commerce International Bank.

There's an abundance of battered yellow cabs, 'smartened up' with gaudy tinsel. It's best to establish the fare first. As a rough guide from the Hilton Hotel to the airport should cost about £S2. Tipping is not expected. For a lower fare cabbies at the box terminals will take five people travelling in the same direction.

Moving on

Buy your bus tickets from the place of departure — preferably a day in advance. **Souk Shaby** and **Souk Saggana** (both about a fifteen minute box ride from Souk Arabi) are two departure points for buses and lorries; neither has recognized accommodation. Remember prices and the duration of the journey depend on conditions — the weather, the driver, breakdowns, inflation — all of them are unpredictable in Sudan.

Travelling north

Lorries leave almost daily for **Dongola** from the post office square in Omdurman (a minute's walk from the main souk). The trip costs £S8 and takes a day and a half. The excellent Nimeiri Express leaves twice a week from Souk Saggana (£S18, twelve hours). A couple of old country buses also make the trip every week (£S12, a day and a half).

Lorries and buses leave for **Karima** several times a week from the post office square in Omdurman. The trip costs £S6 and takes a day. The train to Karima leaves Khartoum at 7.50 am on Sunday and Wednesday. The journey takes thirty hours.

The train to **Wadi Halfa** leaves Khartoum at 6.40 am on Sunday and Wednesday. The journey takes about thirty hours.

Buses leave daily for **Shendi** from near the railway station in Khartoum North (£S1.75, five hours).

Travelling east

There are at least two buses a day leaving from Souk Shaby to each of the destinations below. Travelling is on the excellent new asphalt road, so delays are minimal.

The fare to **Kassala** is £S7 and the journey takes eight hours; to **Gadaref** it's £S4 and takes five hours. Passengers for **Pt Sudan** should change at Kassala.

There's an hourly service to **Wad Medani** so reservations are not necessary. The fare is £S2; the journey takes two hours.

Lorries from the lorry park at Souk Shaby leave to the above destinations for a lower fare. You can sometimes catch a lorry from Souk Arabi in the town centre.

The Khartoum to Kassala train (a thirty-hour journey) leaves on Thursday at 1.30 p.m, however the bus journey is recommended in preference.

The train to Pt Sudan leaves at 7.45 pm on Tuesday and Thursday; the journey takes twenty-seven hours, via Atbara. The bus journey, via Kassala, is less tiring.

Travelling south

To **Kosti** it's a seven-hour journey along the dusty, semi-desert Nile route. At least two buses (fare: £S6) and several lorries depart each day from Souk Shaby. Lorries also leave from Souk Arabi and the Hilal Stadium in Omdurman. All the trains to the West go via Kosti.

There are regular buses to **Sennar:** £S3 3-hours.

The road from Kosti to **Juba** is closed during the rainy season (May to mid November). In the dry months there are usually direct lorries to Juba from Souk Shaby and occasionally from Souk Arabi. Failing that change at Kosti. The trip to Juba costs £S20 and takes four days.

If there are no direct lorries to **Kadougli** from Souk Shaby or Souk Arabi, change at Kosti. Alternatively go to El Obeid or Debibat and take a lorry or bus.

Dervish Dancing, Omdurman: Dervish dancing is held every Friday afternoon in honour of the revered Hamed El Nil. Though foreigners are perfectly welcome to attend — and even participate — this is certainly not a 'traditional ethnic dance show' put on for the benefit of tourists.

Travelling west

Most road transport leaves from Omdurman, some from Souk Arabi. Lorries to the following places leave from around the Hilal Stadium, a five-minute walk to the west of Omdurman's main souk.

Lorries to **El Fasher** travel via El Nahud (£S15, five days). Lorries sometimes leave from the Libyan souk near the camel market.

The trip to **Nyala** costs £S15 and takes five days; to **Barbanousa** £S10, four days; and to **El Obeid** £S6, two days. There's also a daily bus to **El Obeid,** £S10 one day.

At present there is only one train a week to Nyala and **Wau.** Both travel as far as Barbanousa (a three-day journey via Kosti, Er Rahad and Debibat) before going separate ways. The Khartoum to Nyala train leaves at 10.30 am on Monday and takes four or five days. The Wau train leaves at 10.30 am on Wednesday and also takes four or five days. Trains bound for El Obeid leave on three evenings a week, the journey takes twenty-four hours.

Flying Out of Khartoum

The airport is situated 5 km S.E. of City Centre.

When you buy an international airline ticket, you must have proof that you have changed the price of the ticket from foreign currency into Sudanese pounds at the Bank of Sudan.

The following fares are one way (in pounds sterling):
Khartoum to London £280 (£225 under-26 youth fare), to Cairo £60, to Nairobi £160.

There are daily flights to Europe, the Middle East and important African cities.

Passengers departing from Khartoum on an international flight are charged £S4 airport tax.

6 To The South & West

Khartoum to Kosti

The direct route along the Nile passes through drab semi desert. The new road is in the process of being tarmacked. At present it's a seven-hour journey by bus or lorry, twelve hours by train.

Kosti

Kosti (named after a Greek shopkeeper who once lived here) developed at the bridging point when the railway extension was constructed to El Obeid in 1911. Today it is one of the fastest growing towns in Sudan: It has become the northern terminus for river traffic travelling to and from the South, and the cross-roads for east and west land transport, especially since the completion of the beautiful $20 m Kosti Bridge. Kenana sugar plant, a half-hour drive away, has just opened. An oil refinery is being built outside the town and other schemes — equally incongruous to the sparse area — are in the pipeline. There is a feeling that Kosti has outgrown the 'quaint market-town' stage: the souk has sprawled over the usual defined limits and is busier than in other towns — which is quite an attraction. The population is very mixed, West Africans probably make up the highest proportion of foreign immigrants.

Where to stay and eat

A ten-minute walk from the station are three neighbouring hotels. The establishment on the corner is £S1 a night, the other two, at £S1.50, are cleaner. The café opposite is small, pleasantly quiet and open until late.

The rest house — a recently converted colonial bungalow, set in a peaceful, well kept garden — is around £S10 a night.

There are a couple of cheap run down hotels by the football stadium. Many people sleep in the open behind the station.

Around the souk are many cafés and juice bars.

Kosti Railway Station: At most stations locals sell tea, fruit and an assortment of other refreshments — depending on the size of the town. Their timetable is not regulated to the time of day, but rather to that of the trains.

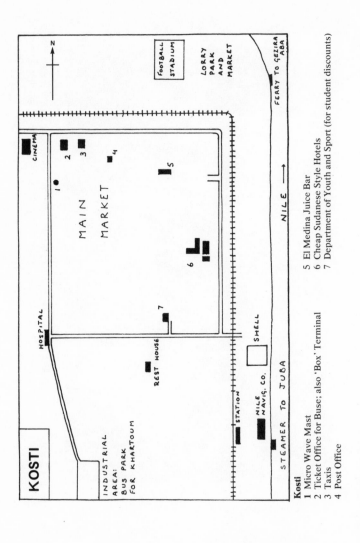

Kosti

1 Micro Wave Mast
2 Ticket Office for Buses; also 'Box' Terminal
3 Taxis
4 Post Office
5 El Medina Juice Bar
6 Cheap Sudanese Style Hotels
7 Department of Youth and Sport (for student discounts)

A typical Sudanese style hotel, Kosti: The Lakonda — Sudanese style hotel — is often the only type of accommodation to be found outside Khartoum and Port Sudan. Within their walls little more than a bed — often the courtyard — and washing facilities are provided. They are generally clean and quite adequate for most peoples' wishes.

Aba Gezira, near Kosti: The everpresent tea ladies are often the only source of refreshments outside the towns and villages. On their stoves made from old tin containers and fuelled by charcoal, they brew up the strong, black and very sweet tea which is drunk throughout the country.

168

Gezira Aba

This town is where Mohammed Ahmed spent time in religious contemplation and built up his reputation as the Mahdi. It has few outstanding features but is a centre for Mahdism. Gezira Aba is a short bus ride from the landing point for ferries crossing the Nile.

Moving on

By Boat

At the moment only one steamer plies the route from Kosti to **Juba.** It is antiquated — like those on Lake Aswan — with a barge strapped to either side (one for first-class passengers, the other for second-class). At the front are three more barges; these not only carry third class passengers but also act as barrages against floating debris in the Sudd. (A new luxury boat is due to come into service in the near future).

The boat is packed, particularly during the Rains (May to mid November), when the Kosti-Juba road is impassable.

Water on board is pumped from the Nile. You'd be wise to take your own drinking vessel and water-purifying tablets. Some passengers swim from the boat; there's less chance of contracting bilharzia if you swim in the middle of the river, where the water is reasonably fast flowing, than near the banks.

The **Sudd,** swampland between **Malakal** and **Bor,** has been called a 'damp hell for men, and a haven for mosquitoes'. You can buy mosquito coils and nets in Khartoum.

The journey upstream takes about twelve days. A few love it; most find it unbearably long. It takes about a week to travel downstream — a tolerable trip.

According to the timetable the steamer leaves Kosti every Tuesday. However, in practice the boat arrives when it arrives and leaves when it leaves. Most people waiting for the boat at Kosti camp free of charge in the area between the station and the wharf. I met families there who had been waiting two weeks.

Having said that, if you are in Khartoum keep in touch with the Railway Enquiries Office (open twenty-four hours a day) at the station (tel: 71133/75388). Nile Navigation gives them twenty-four hours' notice when a boat is due, which gives the office time to broadcast the news and arrange a special train to ferry passengers to Kosti.

There are only a half dozen or so first- and second-class cabins, each with one or two bunks. These are basic but private. The rest of the cabins are used by the crew. So few cabins are

The Kosti-Juba steamer: Barges are attached on either side and in front of the steamer to provide extra accommodation for passengers and goods. During the Rains these vessels are the only means of transport direct from Kosti to the south.

allocated to the passengers as the rich can afford to fly and won't put up with an unreliable and lengthy journey. However, cabins should still be booked in advance. There are basic shower and toilet facilities for all classes (including third).

Most overland travellers opt for the cramped and somewhat squalid conditions of third class. The barge's flat roof provides protection against sun and rain and also acts as an extra deck — a refuge from the crowds. Try and secure a place as soon as the boat arrives at Kosti (or Juba if you are travelling from the South).

Fares are: £S50, first class; £S36, second class; £S16 third class. Students are eligible for half-price travel in second and third class, obtainable in the same way as a railway discount warrant (see p. 107).

The restaurant on board is generally used only by first- and second-class passengers as the prices are comparatively high. For around £S2 you get a three-course meal comprised of eggs, soup or ful or meat and pudding. Don't expect to be able to buy food en route (except at Malakal and Bor). Most third-class passengers take provisions (all obtainable in Kosti): a stove made from an old tin container costs about £S1, a week's supply of charcoal is another £S1, and pots and pans can be bought for a couple of pounds. Butane Gaz is difficult to get in Sudan.

Other transport and destinations

There is a certain romanticism about taking a boat up the Nile. However, once you have waited at Kosti for a couple of weeks and the boat has still not materialized, this wears off. You can take a lorry direct to Juba in the dry season. (A longer, but very worthwhile alternative, is to go west then south, see p. 177).

The road to **Juba** is closed from May to mid November. Lorry fares vary between £S10 and £S20 depending on your bargaining ability and the driver's generosity. Assuming there are no hitches the trip should take three to four days. However, just south of Malakel you have to cross the River Sobat on a rather dilapidated ferry. If it has broken down or there is a queue, you just have to wait your turn: a normal delay of a few hours has been known to develop into days. The journey is through the flat Dinka, Shilluk and Nuer territories.

Several passenger trains pass through Kosti each week; three to **El Obeid,** one to **Nyala** and one to **Wau** — all travelling to or from **Khartoum.** There is also a train to meet the Juba ferry.

Lorries — and some buses — to most parts of the country mainly leave from the area between the football stadium and the vegetable market. Fares (and the duration of the journey) to some of the main destinations are: Nyala — £S10, four days; El Obeid — £S3, one day; Kadougli — £S5, a day and a half; Juba — £S15, three and a half days; Khartoum — £S5, seven hours.

At least two buses each morning leave from the industrial area bound for Khartoum; price; £S6. Ticket stalls are near the cinema.

Fishermen on the Nile, Kosti: Fishing on the Nile is not practised on a large commercial scale. Practices vary from region to region, but commonly a net is cast from a small boat or from the banks of the river.

The Kosti to Juba boat trip

The steamer is too wide to fit through the pillars of the railway bridge a few kilometres south of Kosti; so the barges are unstrapped, pulled through individually by a tug, and strung together again the other side. The whole procedure takes about four hours. Kosti is the last bridging point on the Nile until Juba 1500km upstream.

The atmosphere of the steamer resembles something out of Conrad's Heart of Darkness. Brass plaques request passengers not to wear pyjamas for dinner, while others list acceptable evening attire. Despite these charms, the steamers relegation to the scrapyard is long overdue.

As the boat chugs into Upper Nile Province the scrub desert slowly transforms into equally flat bush grass. This is the northern edge of the Tioc, which in Dinka means 'grazing land flooded annually, but yellow in the dry season'.

Towards the end of the last century, European nations — particularly Britain and France — were eager to gain footholds in the Upper Nile valley. In 1895 Britain, who felt she had a certain right to the territory, declared that she would regard any intrusion by another nation into the Upper Nile as an 'unfriendly act'. This declaration was directed particularly at France.

At this time Sudan belonged to the Khalifa and the Mahdists; further north in Egypt, Kitchener was amassing Anglo-Egyptian forces before moving south to conquer Sudan. On 18th September 1896 a small mission of ten French officers and 150 Senegalese riflemen left Loanga (French Congo) under the command of Captain Jean Baptiste Marchand. Their intention was to plant their flag 2,500 km north east at the small town of **Fashoda** (by present-day Kodok) on the west bank of the Nile, thus establishing a French claim to the area. Marchand's truly heroic journey took his mission up the Congo River and across uncharted swamps and plains. His troops battled against disease, hostile tribes, poor supplies, seasonal rivers, extreme weather conditions and treacherous terrain. On 10th July 1898 they arrived at Fashoda, remarkably without a single death.

Fashoda was 'nothing but a mass of bricks and mud', according to Dr. Emily, a member of the expedition. The French flag was hoisted and fortifications were built. While Marchand awaited further orders from Paris, he drew up a treaty with the local Shilluk chief, who was fed up with paying tribute to the Mahdists, and established the area as a French protectorate.

173

The new bridge, Kosti: Incongruous in its sparse and undeveloped surroundings, the new Kosti bridge - at the time of writing it's linked at either bank by a dirt track — is the last bridging point until Juba.

174

Meanwhile Kitchener had won successive battles against the Mahdists in the north, and on 4th September, after his victory at Omdurman, he inaugurated the Anglo-Egyptian Condominium in Khartoum. He immediately moved south to meet Marchand. Their meeting was businesslike, though polite, and they praised each other's accomplishments. Kitchener stated that Sudan was now under the control of the Anglo-Egyptian government. Marchand replied that he would stay put until he received directions from France.

In Europe it seemed a major war was imminent. Britain's Daily Mail damned Marchand's men as 'scum of the desert' and 'mere tourists'. The French Prime Minister retorted saying he 'would rather accept war than submit'.

However, the French government, fearing they would suffer badly in a war with Britain, quietly told Marchand to pack up and come home. So, without a drop of blood spilt, the Fashoda Incident ended, leaving the Anglo-Egyptian Condominium in control of Sudan and the Upper Nile.

Malakal, just north of the River Sobat, is the last town until past the Sudd (in Arabic sudd means barrage) and the centre for the Shilluk. In dugouts lone Shilluk drift along the sides of the river, stabbing the banks with their spears; their endeavours are occasionally rewarded with a mudfish.

It takes about a week to get through the **Sudd** upstream (four days downstream); during the floods this route is equal to the length of Britain. The novelty of the swamp rapidly wears off, replaced by the tedium of continuously pushing aside floating clumps of papyrus. However, the Sudd is an ornithologists paradise (as is most of the South) with thousands of exotic birds, some unique to Sudan. Wildlife is plentiful, though whether you see the crocodiles, hippos, lions and giraffes which are reputed to be along the banks is a matter of chance.

About 80 kms north of **Bor,** which marks the end of the Sudd, is the head regulator of the Jonglei canal. At present the Upper Nile loses half it's waters in the Sudd through evaporation and transpiration. When finished, the canal (which ends just south of Malakel) will minimize floods, reduce evaporation, provide better transport and control irrigation.

From Bor it's just over 165 kms to **Juba** in Eastern Equatoria.

Train near El Obeid: Old British steam engines still operate on some of the train services. Kitchener, as commander of the Anglo-Egyptian forces, pioneered Sudan's railway system to help him reconquer the country at the end of the last century.

The new boat

When the new boat comes into service, it will supposedly take only five days to complete the journey upstream to Juba and three days back downstream. Hopefully, the timetable will also be more reliable. Fares are not much higher than those of the old boat: mumtazah class costs £S63 per person in a double cabin; first class £S55 per person, with four in a cabin; second class £S40 per person, with six in a cabin. There are no reductions in any class.

The new boat sounds as if it will provide an excellent service. The old boat will continue to provide a cheap, third class service.

Khartoum to Barbanousa

The three-day train ride from Khartoum to Barbanousa passes through mile after mile of semi desert, which gradually becomes greener with small acacia bushes and baobab trees. A story goes that God, angry with the world, plucked the baobab off the face of the earth and stuck it back upside down — hence its root-like branches. Baobabs have a tremendous ability to store water which can easily be tapped during the dry season. In Kenya the elephants do this by goring the trunk with their tusks.

El Obeid

El Obeid, Kordofan's important market town and administrative centre, is the world's centre for gum arabic. In 1883, after a seige of several months, it was the first town to fall to the Mahdi. A 10,000-man Egyptian army was sent under British commander William Hicks to recapture the town. However, it was completely annihilated by the Mahdi — a tremendous psychological and strategic victory.

El Obeid is a bustling but intimate town — an interesting place to stay a night or two if you happen to be passing that way.

The British Council library is near the Catholic Church.

Where to stay and eat

Hotels are scattered around the periphery of the market. The **International** and the **John** (around £S3) are the best in town. The **Arous** (£S1) and the **Shikan** (£S1.50) are the cleanest of the cheaper ones.

Some good cafés skirt the souk.

Tea stall, Kordofan: Those who travel by lorry depend on tea stalls for refreshments and basic meals. The Baobab tree is a great storer of water and is sometimes tapped.

178

Camels watering by the railway track, Kordofan: Modern transport has virtually driven the traditional trading caravans into extinction. However, camels and donkeys are still the most common means of travel for individuals in the north.

Moving on

Lorries travelling west leave daily from near the International hotel. The journey to **Nyala** takes three days and costs £S8.

Buses and lorries travelling south leave every morning from near the Shikan hotel. The trip to **Kadougli** costs £S4 and takes eight hours.

Lorries heading east leave daily from the **mawgif** (lorry park) near the small Abu Jahal souk (a ten-minute walk from the town centre). The fare to **Khartoum** is £S6 and the journey takes two days; **Kosti** £S3, one day. A non-stop bus to Khartoum (duration of journey twenty-four hours) leaves daily from near the International hotel; the fare is £S10

The train from El Obeid to **Khartoum** leaves at 7 am on Monday and Thursday, 10 am on Saturday. The journey takes twenty-four hours. To go west by rail you must catch a train at Er Rahad, a four-hour drive to the south of El Obeid.

Nuba Mountains

The journey from Debitat to Kadougli is 165 km along a tarmac road. During the last few years the Nuba Mountains, with their strange hills and fascinating peoples, have become one of the most documented regions of Sudan. Films and glossy picture books e.g. 'The Last of the Nuba' and 'The People of Kau', for instance, both by Leni Riefenstal, depicting the tribes' ceremonies are, for better or for worse, starting to generate more films and glossy picture books, and to attract travellers. I am reluctant to list the 'beautiful isolated villages' which exist in this area.

Because of the interest shown in the Nuba Mountains, the Commissioner at Kadougli likes all foreigners to register with him.

How to get there

Lorries and buses travel from **El Obeid** to **Kadougli;** the fare is £S4 and the journey takes eight hours. Lorries and buses also leave **Debibat** (located on the railroad) fare £S2, duration three hours.

Vehicles from **Umm Ruwaba** and **Er Rahad** travel to **Kologi** (£S5, six hours) near the Eastern Hills and some of the region's most beautiful coutnryside.

Going south, from **Kadougli** to **Talodi** to **El Liri** to **Malakal** (£S8) takes about a day if the vehicle is going direct.

During the Rains (June to October) travelling in the region can be extremely difficult — sometimes impossible. It is often only possible to get from one village to another by foot.

Barbanousa

Situated at the East-West-South road and rail junction, Barbanousa is an important transit point. The large lorry park just off the market is a five minute walk from the station; there are a couple of hotels on the way.

There are oil rigs in the region and there is talk of building a refinery, probably near Barbanousa.

Barbanousa to Nyala

It is a day's journey by train from Barbanousa to **Nyala**, passing through Ed Da'ein. Transport can be seriously affected by the Rains.

Train between Barbanousa and Nyala: The railway system, in a country where travel is difficult, distances are long and all weather roads are few, is the important backbone to Sudan's communications.

Nyala

The most westerly province of Darfur was always regarded as isolated from the rest of Sudan. It retained a high degree of independence: Islam didn't reach here until the seventeenth century, and during the Condominium it had its own Sultanate which lasted until 1916, when Ali Dinar (the last Sultan) was defeated by the Anglo Egyptian forces.

The railway reached the town of Nyala in 1960. This opened up the region and has subsequently made it the terminus and market for all imports and exports to and from the area. European construction companies are building an asphalt road to Zolengei with the intention of developing Jebel Marra's orchards.

In size, purpose and even atmosphere, Nyala falls somewhere between Kassala and Kosti. The large market, with a reasonable selection of handicrafts, dominates the sprawling town.

A typical general store, Nyala: Towns and most villages have adequate food supplies. Towns usually have several reasonably stocked general stores, depending on their accessibility to the main transport routes. However, most of their goods are of little use to the average person. Tinned food is more expensive than in Europe.

Where to stay and eat

Three quarters of the way into town from the station is the **Darfur Hotel:** 25PT to sleep on the roof or in a dormitory, £S1 for a single room. If you are making a round trip to Jebel Marra, the hotel will look after any luggage you want to leave behind. Next to the government buildings, by the microwave mast, is the rest house: £S7 for full board.

There's the usual abundance of cheap eating places in the market. On the way into the centre from the Darfur Hotel are a couple of above-average juice bars and cafés.

The tourist and registration offices are among the government buildings beyond the microwave mast.

Moving on

Occasionally travellers en route for Jebel Marra and with a lot of time on their hands buy a donkey from the animal market at Nyala for about £S40. Someone from the Tourist Office will help you select and bargain for your beast. Camels and horses are far more expensive. However, before you spend your money on a donkey, find out whether fodder is readily available and where and for how much you can expect to resell your animal.

Lorries travelling east leave from near the Bank of Sudan every day (there are fewer in the rainy season). The trip to **Barbanousa** costs £S5 and takes a day and a half; to **El Obeid** £S8, three days; **Khartoum** £S15, five days.

The station is two kilometres from the town centre. The journey from Nyala to **Khartoum** takes five or six days; the train leaves at 6 pm on Thursday.

Lorries for **Jebel Marra** leave from Souk Um Dafaso (a section of the main market beyond the rest house). **Nyertiti** is an overnight journey away (£S3); lorries leave every evening except Friday. Lorries for **Dribat** and **Gorlangbang** leave once a week; for **Zolengi** and **Genena** fairly frequently (from the football stadium).

For **Wau,** take a train or lorry to Barbanousa and — hopefully — meet the Khartoum to Wau train (there is no official connection). During the dry season there are lorries which take four days and charge £S10.

Buses leave daily for **El Fasher** from near the football stadium (fare £S6; duration eight hours).

Several lorries a week (from December to May) leave for **Bangui, CAR.** The fare is £S40, and the journey takes eight days (from Souk Um Dafaso).

El Fasher

Founded in 1700, El Fasher became the starting point for the Darb El Arbain (see below) after the decline of nearby Kobbe. Formerly it was the seat of the Sultanate and is now capital of the province though it's not such an important market town as Nyala. There are frequent buses and lorries to both Khartoum and Nyala.

Darb El Arbain (the forty-day route), so called because of the time it takes to cover its 1,600 km by camel, is one of Africa's oldest and most famous caravan routes. Caravans used to start from Kobbe and make their way north through the Libyan Desert, via the oasis of Selima, to Assyut in Egypt. An eighteenth-century European traveller estimated there was £115,000 worth of merchandise on one such journey; two thousand camels in a caravan was quite normal. Slaves, ivory and rhino horns from the south would be traded for cotton, beads, silks and soap from Egypt.

Jebel Marra

Jebel Marra, a range of hills 55 km from east to west and 65 km from north to south and about 140 km north west of Nyala is regarded as one of Sudan's notable tourist attractions. However, during a week of walking around the area, I did not come across another foreigner or tourist.

Sudanese talk of Jebel Marra with great affection and intimacy. In mouth watering detail they describe the abundant orchards laden with mangoes, oranges, grapefruit, and guavas. Then there are the waterfalls, the **Deriba Lakes** (the lakes in the crater of Mt Gimbala), the favourable climate and, of course, the greenness. Yet it is surprising how few have actually visited this paradise.

Consequently few of the stories you hear about Jebel Marra are first hand. Facts have become fantastic tales as they have been related by one person to another: if a bird other than an eagle flies across the smaller crater lake, gravitational pull will suck it down to its death; a person swimming in the lake will suffer a similar peril; the people of the crater (many have never ventured outside the mountain walls) often live to 150 years; lions gobble up lone travellers after dark. Somtimes it's difficult to know what to believe; however when you are travelling off the beaten track do not dismiss the advice of locals lightly.

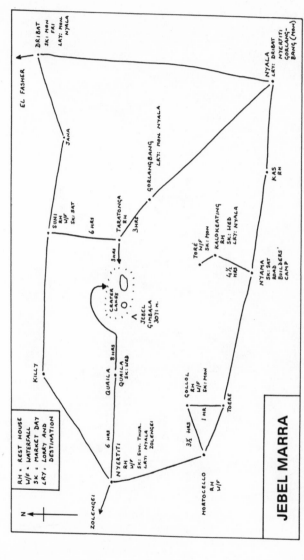

JEBEL MARRA

Map legend (boxed):
R.H. = REST HOUSE
W/F = WATERFALL
SK = MARKET DAY
LRY = LORRY AND DESTINATION

Map labels:

EL FASHER

DRIBAT
SK: MON.
FRI.
LRY: MON.
NYALA

JANA

SUNI
R.H.
W/F
SK: SAT

KILLY

QUAILA 8 HRS
QUAILA
SK: WED

6 HRS

CRATER LAKES

JEBEL GIMBALA 3071 m.

TARATONGA
R.H.
3 HRS

GORLANGBANG
LRY: MON. NYALA

NYERTITI
R.H.
W/F
SK: SUN. THUR.
LRY: NYALA
ZOLENGEI

6 HRS

GOLLOL
R.H.
W/F
SK: MON

1 HR

TOERE

3½ HRS

MORTOCELLO
R.H.
W/F

ZOLENGEI

N

TORÉ
W/F
SK: MON

KALOKEATING
R.H.
SK: WED
LRY: NYALA

4½ HRS

NYAMA
SK: SAT
AND
BUILDERS'
CAMP

KAS
R.H.

NYALA
LRY: DRIBAT
NYERTITI
GORLANG-
BANG (NYER.)

I copied this map from an anonymous American - to whom I'm very grateful - who had travelled extensively around Jebel Marra. There isn't an official map of this area, he drew this one with help from locals. It should be treated purely as a rough. The times refer to how long it takes to get from one place to the next on foot.

185

Niertiti: One of the main villages in Jebel Marra. Market day is twice a week when people from the neighbouring homesteads — sometimes half a day's donkey ride away — will come to buy and sell goods. If you want to reach the crater lakes, market day is the time to find someone returning home in that direction.

186

A village near Niertiti: There are now plans to develop Jebel Marra's orchards on a commercial scale. An all weather highway is being constructed by German contractors which will pass near this village.

The crater floor, Jebel Marra: The first impression as you look from the crest down onto the crater floor is that there is no life here, except for the eagle like birds which continually encircle the 'male' lake. Once you have descended, though, you gradually pick out the occasional stone hut, camouflaged against the crater walls, the fine horses roaming the pasture and the occasional person herding a few goats or collecting salt from the shores of the 'female' lake.

Getting to the Deriba Lakes

From **Nyala** there are lorries to **Nyertiti**, **Zolengei**, and **Gorlangbang**. The only way to travel around the rest of Jebel Marra is by foot or on donkey, horse or camel.

The two main routes to the lakes are from Nyertiti and Taratonga — a far easier walk. The approach is a gradual ascent up a series of plateaux, dissected by deep ravines which contain streams only during the rainy season. At Quaila I found a guide for £S8 (just ask around) to take me to the lakes. We took a day to reach our goal, spent a night in the crater and another day returning. He provided a donkey for our bags, some food and ample marisa (beer) when we got back to his home. Without him I would never have found my way. During our two-day journey we passed only three people — none of whom could have explained the route to me had I been alone. There was no food along the way and, as it was April, only a couple of springs.

The Deriba Lakes

The crater, 5 by 6½ km and 1,400 m above sea level (510 m above the plains) has a gap in its eastern wall. There are only a couple of other safe routes to descend to the lakes.

The big, shallow lake (the 'female'), with it's salt-encrusted banks, has salty water, though there is a small spring at its south-east corner. The water of the smaller, very deep 'male' lake (in its own perfect crater) tastes of sulphur. There are pastures where inhabitants graze their goats and let loose their fine horses. At night the surrounding mountain walls help create an eerie lunar atmosphere.

Towns and villages

Most places on the perimeter of the map have orchards. **Nyertiti**, where large scale market gardens are in their infancy, and **Sunni,** the only place in Jebel Marra with electricity, are the two towns in the region that have basic shops and cafés. Both are beautiful. Except in these towns you cannot expect to find food other than on market days. You can stay without permission at most rest houses, which provide little more than a shelter.

Barbanousa to Wau

The railway was extended to **Wau** in 1962, providing an important link to the South. Along with the Nile steamers it acts as the means of transport from the North to South during the Rains.

What is interesting about this two-day journey is the transition from Arab to Black, and patchy scrub to rich greenery. Villages and a few small towns have grown up along the tracks.

A village between Barbanousa and Wau: At the beginning of the 1960s the railway was extended to Wau in the south, many villages and homesteads evolved alongside the track. Interesting is the transition to Negro cultures and exuberant vegetation as the journey proceeds.

7 The South

'The real Sudan lies far to the south — moist, undulating and exuberant.'

Winston Churchill

The Sudan is divided into the North and the South geographically, historically, culturally, and politically. On maps the border is shown roughly following the 10° N parallel, except at the Nile where it is further north at Renk.

In the mid-nineteenth century, slavery reached it's peak: 50,000 slaves a year were brought down from Upper Nile. Foreigners and Northern slave-traders sent caravans to the Black South and robbed villages of their finest men, women and children. The trade died at the end of the last century, but the horrendous damage had been done and lived for long in the memories of the Southerners.

Under the Condominium the South developed independently of the North. Its a moot point whether the British really had plans to affiliate the region to Uganda and Kenya because they realised that the cultural affinity of the South was there, rather than with the Islamic North. At any rate, Arab customs and language were discouraged in favour of English or tribal tongues; Arab officials were replaced, and passports were necessary for movement between the two regions. The aim was to rid the South of Arab influence.

After the Second World War the outlook changed and it was agreed that the North and the South should unite. However, in 1955 the Equatorial Corps, fearing Arab domination after independence, mutinied against their Northern officers. This began a seventeen-year North-South civil war which resulted in an exodus of Southerners to neighbouring countries, the destruction of communications, the crippling of the Southern economy and the formation of the Southern Anya-Nya ('snake-venom') geurilla organization. Five hundred thousand people died in the war.

On coming to power, Nimeiri granted the South regional autonomy, which came into force after the Addis Ababa Agreement in 1972. The South was able to develop in its own way and was granted budgets for economy and education, yet remained within a united Sudan.

Travelling in the South

People in the South are more sensitive to foreigners than those in the North. It's imperative that your registration and travel permits are in order.

At present the political situation along the southern border is volatile and extremely unpredictable. Some travellers passing through Uganda have been robbed by soldiers; others come back with glowing reports of hospitality. Western embassies in Khartoum will tell you what is happening in the region, but don't be too put off by 'behind-the-desk' officials who, as a matter of course, warn you against travelling here. The most accurate information is from other travellers. Do, however, use your own discretion.

Wau

Wau is the capital of Bhar El Ghazal region. During the last century, slave-traders, such as the famous Zubhair Rahma, lived like lords on vast estates and exploited the 'Black Ivory'.

With the railway, Wau has grown rapidly and is better stocked with food and general supplies than Juba. The market sells a variety of handicrafts and is a centre for the Dinka and other south-western tribes. At the far end smithies salvage girders and odds and ends of old trucks: a spear or arrow head beaten from a leaf spring commands the highest prices because of the extra strength of the iron. Wood — ebony, mahogany, teak, vuba — is the main resource of the region.

The Jur, Wau's river, is navigable downstream from August to October, though passenger steamers are not in operation.

It's important to get travel permits and to register at the main police headquarters (fairly near the youth hostel). The Youth and Sport Centre — for student rail warrants — is towards the Cathedral from the town centre.

Where to stay and eat

The **Youth Hostel** is about five minutes' walk from the market. It's rather run down, but almost every room has its own shower — for 25PT you can't complain. **El Nilein**, near the hostel charges £S2 and has a restaurant that's open until late. **Barbara** is the best hotel in town (around £S6 a head).

There are a couple of rest houses, but these are usually reserved for government officials.

The **Unity Restaurant** is one of the better eating places in town.

On the Rumbeck road (near Juba) between Wau and Juba: The south is characterised by luxuriant equatorial vegetation and heavy rains. Thick, tall grasses alongside the roads often limit panoramic viewpoints to the top of the lorries.

Moving on

The train to **Khartoum** leaves Wau at 10 am on Saturday and covers the distance in four to five days.

The lorry park is near the satellite-tracking station. Lorries travel to **Barbanousa** only in the dry season.

For **CAR** you could try catching a vehicle from Tambura, 250 km south of Wau near the border. Vehicles for **Zaire** also leave from Tambura and then go to Iso on the border. Alternatively, you can get transport further to the east from Yei, six hours south west of Juba.

A mail truck leaves for **Juba** once or twice a week from behind the youth hostel. It's usually free for students — though this is not a hard-and-fast rule.

The Southern roads have a harder surface and are better defined than most of those in the North. The problem is that the Rains can have a disastrous effect on them. I travelled the Rumbeck road from Juba to Wau in October. For two consecutive nights it rained heavily, leaving murky pools of water twenty to thirty metres long in the middle of the road. At times one side of our path was level, while the other side was a huge hole, which meant the lorry had to tilt — at times almost forty-five degrees — and inch precariously through the hazard. One time the truck boy was told to test the depth of one of these 'puddles'. He was about 5 ft 10 ins; by the time he had waded to the middle, the water was up to his shoulders. The next few hours were spent filling the hole with rocks and anything else we could lay our hands on. That day we covered only 25 km in over twelve hours.

On the Rumbeck road between Wau and Juba: The Rains can have a disastrous affect on the conditions of the roads in the south. A lorry may get stuck, block the road and cause a dozen other vehicles to wait until its dug its way out. Unlike the north the roads are cut through thick vegetation, so vehicles are restricted to this path. An all weather road is planned along this route.

Wau to Juba

The Northern Rumbeck Road

The road, pockmarked with pot-holes passes over the flat marshlands of the Southern Clay Plains. It's not a particularly scenic route, but the homesteads that cut into the tall grass by the side of the road are fascinating. The archetypal African huts (sometimes raised on stilts), made from sticks, straw, leaves or mud with their flattened conical roofs, cluster around a large, luxuriant tree on a patch of cleared earth. In varying degrees this is a feature throughout the South. Dinka are predominant along the route. Clothes, if any, are minimal; men often carry no more than their spears, and women a water-container — plastic 'jerry cans' of all sizes are prize possessions.

Honey is gathered daily and mixed with fermenting durra, the result is an extremely thirst-quenching beer. Despite the high rainfall fresh water and food is scarce.

There are a couple of towns — **Tonj** and **Rumbeck,** both are interesting, with markets and medical aid. Other villages, until **Amadi**, have police posts but little else.

The lorry fare is £S15, and the journey takes two or three days.

The Southern Zande road

I have never travelled the Southern road, but from all accounts it's far more beautiful than the Rumbeck route. Sometimes called the Zande road, after the Azande who occupy the southwest corner of Sudan, it's in hillier terrain so doesn't have a great drainage problem; however, long hold-ups are caused by the washing away of bridges.

Much of the journey is along the Zaire border. Fruits and wildlife are abundant and big-game hunters are said to pay $3,000 a week to try to shoot a few elephant.

Nzara, **Yambio** and **Maridi** are particularly attractive places. The lorry fare is £S20, and the journey takes four days.

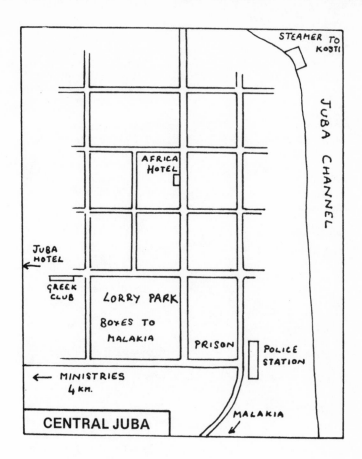

CENTRAL JUBA

Juba

Juba is the last navigable point on the Nile. As yet its rather shabby downtown doesn't reflect Juba's importance as the Southern capital. During the Rains the oppressive climate and malarial air make you sympathise with nineteenth-century pioneers who, based across the river at Old Gondokoro, suffered similar conditions.

Ministries, business headquarters and a new university are some of the signs of the South's plans for independent development.

During the frequent petrol shortages Juba becomes a bottleneck of frustrated travellers searching for a vehicle: take any transport going your way — it may be a long time before the next lift.

Where to Stay

The **Africa Hotel** is the only hotel that caters for travellers. Unlike most of Sudan's hotels, the Africa is squalid. Beds are from 80PT a night.

The **Juba Hotel** is an old British establishment, now run by the Ministry of Tourism but still retaining much of its original style. A single room costs £S20.

Sometimes various missionaries and institutes let out rooms. However, camping at the police station is the most popular form of accommodation with travellers. Government rest houses are only for official use at the moment, but it is thought this will change.

Where to Eat

There are several restaurants around the town, though food isn't abundant. The restaurant at the **Africa Hotel** is quite good: their yoghurt is a speciality. The **People's Restaurant** serves stuffed aubergine and is considered one of the best eating places in town. The **Arizona** is of much the same standard. A three-course meal at the **Juba Hotel** costs around £S5.

The **Greek Club** with its mining-town saloon-cum-restaurant atmosphere, is the hub of Juba's evening life. It serves a variety of reasonably priced dishes and sells beer. It's open until 11 pm.

What to Do

There is Dinka dancing on some evenings — just follow the singing to find out where. A new cultural centre has opened, there are displays and shows most evenings.

Klony Klony, the well known market in Malakia, has a good selection of handicrafts, fruit stalls and cheap restaurants. Its a half-hour walk from the town centre, or you can take a box or bus from the lorry park.

Permits

Southerners are particular about documents being in order. Permits issued in the North can be invalid in the South. Register and obtain travel permits at the police station.

Photo permits are available from the Ministry of Information (about three km from the town centre).

With its Christian influence the South's Sunday is a 'day of worship' rather than Friday; however, main Islamic holidays are respected.

Moving On

Ask around ministries, relief organizations, missions, merchants — in fact anybody — for lifts. It's quite common to hitch a plane ride anywhere around the country or even to Kenya. There are scheduled flights to Khartoum and Nairobi.

Lorries to Kenya and Uganda have to be checked at the clearing agent near the Africa hotel, so this is a good place to arrange a lift and buy Kenyan shillings. After checking, lorry drivers often spend the night at Malakia. Also try the Interfreight trucking company behind the Greek Club.

There are passport checks every time you cross the bridge.

The Juba to **Nairobi** trip costs £S25 and takes three or four days (via Uganda or directly to Kenya).

Ask at the lorry park for lifts to **Wau.** If you travel via the Rumbeck road the trip costs £S15 and takes two or three days, via the Zande road £S20, four days.

There is a bus to **Maridi** two or three times a week.

Ask at the post office about mail trucks.

Lorries leave for **Khartoum** from the lorry park and travel via Malakal and Kosti. The trip costs £S20 and takes four days.

The boat timetable is non existent (see p. 171 for the prices). It takes about a week to reach Kosti.

There are two roads to **Kenya**: either direct from Sudan's south-east corner or via Uganda. Drivers prefer the latter route (provided that Uganda is without political problems) because the road is generally in good condition. The rest house at Nimule (£S3 a night) on the border, is reputed to be one of the best in Sudan.

Juba to Lokichokio

The road passes some of Sudan's greenest and most beautiful countryside, famous for its hills shaped like huge boulders. **Torit**, market town and army base, is the first customs check for Kenya; to the south are the Imatong mountains.

The forestry commission are usually happy to give lifts in their landrovers up to **Katire**; from here it's about 12 kms to Gilo, an old colonial resort 1,800 m above sea level.

The rest house costs £S1 a night, but bring your own food.

During the Rains, travel here is difficult. The road from Torit to **Kapoeta** deteriorates drastically. Furthermore, the recent problems in Uganda and the Karamoja region have had repercussions in Sudan; it is now illegal to travel after dark — a precaution against ambushes — and you must stop at one of the many police posts before sunset.

Kapoeta, rather like something out of a spaghetti Western, is Sudan's frontier town. It has a 'last-town' atmosphere, with groups of people just hanging around. Here you are given an exit stamp and that will probably be the end of the Sudanese formalities.

By now the terrain is already turning to semi-arid scrub land. It's debatable exactly where the borderline between Sudan and Kenya is drawn, but about two thirds of the way along the route to Lokichokio there is a tattered strand of black wire strung between two trees. My driver assured me this was the dividing line between the two nations.

(Route continues in Kenya Section, Chapter 2)

Between Torit and Kapoeta: The area through which this road passes is still unsettled after the troubles in the Karamoja region and Uganda. Vehicles must stop before sunset at one of the many police posts.

Appendix A

Distances Along the Route

	km
Wadi Halfa-Abu Hamed (rail)	370
Abu Hamed-Atbara (rail)	245
Atbara-Khartoum (rail)	314
Wadi Halfa-Dongola (road)	400
Dongola-Karima (river)	280
Dongola-Karima (road - across the desert)	185
Karima-Abu Hamed (rail)	248
Dongola-Khartoum (road)	570
Atbara-Pt Sudan (rail)	476
Pt Sudan-Suakin (road)	60
Suakin-Kassala (road)	362
Kassala-Khartoum (road)	387
Khartoum-Kosti (road)	325
Kosti-Renk (river)	174
Renk-Kodok (river)	260
Kodok-Malakal (river)	65
Malakal-Adok (river)	360
Adok-Bor (river)	405
Bor-Juba (river)	165
Khartoum-Er Rahad (rail)	622
Er Rahad-El Obeid (rail)	70
Er Rahad-Debibat (rail)	102
Debibat-Kadugli (road)	165
Debibat-Barbanousa (rail)	245
Barbanousa-Nyala (rail)	350
Barbanousa-Wau (rail)	460
Wau-Juba (road, via Rumbeck)	800
Wau-Juba (road, via the Zande route)	1045
Juba-Nimule (road)	196
Juba-Torit (road)	135
Torit-Kapoeta (road)	177

Appendix B

Some Useful Words and Phrases

Sudanese Arabic varies a little from Egyptian Arabic.

Greetings (peace be with you)	**as salaam alaikum**
(reply)	**wa alaikum as salaam**
Welcome	**ahlan wa sahlan**
Hello	**zayak**
Goodbye	**ma'al salaama**
How are you?	**keifhalek?**
Fine, well	**kways**
Good morning	**sabah al kahair**
Good evening	**misaa al kahair**
Good night	**tasbih al kahair**
Praise be to God, the lord of all the worlds	**el hamdulillah rab el alamin**
Yes	**aywa or nam** (or a click with the side of the tongue).
No	**la**
Please	**mein fadluk**
Thank you	**shukran**
That's all right	**afwan**
It's the will of God (common expression)	**Inshallah**

One	**waahid**	Eleven	**hidaashar**
Two	**ethnain**	Twelve	**etnaashar**
Three	**talaata**	Thirteen	**talataashar**
Four	**arba'a**	Fourteen	**arba'tashar**
Five	**khamsa**	Fifteen	**khamustaashar**
Six	**sitta**	Sixteen	**sittaashar**
Seven	**saba'a**	Seventeen	**saba'taashar**
Eight	**tamaaniya**	Eighteen	**tamantaashar**
Nine	**tisa'a**	Nineteen	**tisa'taashar**
Ten	**a'shara**	Twenty	**a'shreen**

Twenty one	**waahid wa ashreen**
Thirty	**talateen**
Fifty	**khamseen**
Hundred	**miya**
Thousand	**alif**
Today	**alyoum**
Yesterday	**ams**
Tomorrow	**bokura**
Day after tomorrow	**baad bokura**
What time is it?	**al saa a kam?**
Half past five	**khamsa wa nous**
Saturday	**al sabit**
Sunday	**al ahad**
Monday	**al ethnain**
Tuesday	**al thulatha**
Wednesday	**al arbia'a**
Thursday	**al khamees**
Friday	**al jumaa**
Ferry	**bantoun, Moaadia**
Steamer	**baakira**
Bus	**bus**
Lorry	**lorry**
Train	**qattar**
Aeroplane	**taiyara**
Station	**mahatta**
Airport	**mataar**
Lorry park	**mawgif lorry**
Museum	**mathaf**
Hospital	**mustashfa**
Post office	**al busta**
House	**beit**
Hotel	**funduq, lakonda**
Youth Hostel	**beit el shabab**
Square	**midan**
Street	**sharia**
Road	**tareeq**
Market	**souq**
Local market	**souq al arabi**
Electricity	**kahrabaa**
Money	**garoosh**
Change (money)	**fakka**

I	ana
You	inta
He/She	huwa/heeya
We	iyhna
You	intu
They	huma
What is your name?	ismakeh?
My name is …	ana ismakeh …
Do you speak English?	bitkallam ingleezi?
I do not speak Arabic	ana ma bakallim arabi
I do not know	ana ma a'arif
That's fine	kways jiddan
What?	eh?
What is that?	eh da?
What's the matter?	fee eh? malaak?
What do you want?	awiz eh?
Who?	meen?
Why?	lai?
How much?	kam?
I want to go	ana awiz amshi
Where are you going?	marshi wane?
I am going …	ana marshi
I want	ana awiz
I do not want	mish awiz
I am hungry	ana jawa'an
I am thirsty	ana atshan
I like	ana auhib
Go away	imshi
Come here	tafadhl hena
Hurry up	yallah
Stop	agif
Is it possible?	mumkin?
Perhaps	yimkin
…don't you?	…mush kida?
Never mind	malesh
Finished, over	khelas, mafeesh
All of us	kullina
Everything	kullu haga
Here	hena
There	henak
When	emta
After	baad
Later	baadain
Good	kways
Very good	tamaam

Bad	mish kways, battaJ
Hot	harr
Cold	barid
Big	kabeer
Small	saqeer
A lot	kateer
A little	shuwaiya
Expensive	ghali
Cheap	rakhees
Beautiful	gameel
New	jadeed
Boy	walud
Girl	bint
Man	rojul
Woman	mara
Camel	gamel
Donkey	hamar
Coast	shatti
River	nahar
Desert	sahara
Sand	raml
Sea	bhar
Rain	matar
Eat	okul
Restaurant	matam
Bread	aish
Butter	zebda
Cheese	gibna
Eggs	baid
Fish	samak
Fruit	faakha
Meat	lahma
Oil (for cooking)	zaid
Vegetables	khudra
Yoghurt	leban zabadi
Tea	chai
Coffee	kawa
Milk	leban
Water	moya
Visa	tasherat
Embassy	safaara
Department of passports and immigration	maslahat al jawaazat wa al hijra
Ministry of youth	wezara el shabab

Appendix C   Glossary

Ansar — followers of the Madhi

Baksheesh — tip, or some kind of hand-out

Batn el Hagga — the 'Belly of Rocks', a rugged desert region between Wadi Halfa and Dongola

Bilad al sudan — 'land of the Blacks', thus Sudan

Bilharzia — Over half the adult population of Egypt suffer from bilharzia. This disease, which results in the inflammation of the urinary system, is caused by a fluke from the flatworm family.

Eggs which are laid in the blood vessels enter the urinary bladder. They are passed into fresh water where they hatch and attack snails. Here cercariae develop and swim about until they fasten onto mammalian skin (the host). They burrow into the animal's blood vessels and then feed, mature and lay eggs while draining the bowel.

Bilharzia is contracted in slow running waters eg: parts of the Nile and canals

Box — a Toyota pick-up converted into a Sudanese collective taxi

Copt — Egyptian Christian. The word 'copt' means Egypt

Damira — the Nile flood and the cultivating season that follows it

Darb el Arbain — the caravan route from Darfur to Asyut which traditionally takes forty days to complete

Dervish — a member of an Islamic fraternity. The Madhist armies were also known as dervishes

Durra — millet, eaten throughout Sudan

Feddan — a measure of area used in Egypt and Sudan, approximately equal to one acre

Fellahin — the Egyptian peasant farmer

Felucca — the tall-masted river boats used on the Nile in Egypt

Gellabiah — the traditional loose cotton gown worn by Egyptian and Sudanese men

The Gezira — the irrigated region south of Khartoum between the Blue and White Niles. It is here that most of Sudan's cotton is grown

Haboob — dust storm particularly common in April and May in Sudan

Haj — the Muslims' annual pilgrimage to Mecca

Jebel — a hill

Khawaja — a commonly used Sudanese word referring to foreigners

Khor — a temporary stream

The Madhi — Mohammed Ahmed, the religious leader who rose up against the Egyptians in Sudan at the end of the nineteenth century

Nilometer — a gauge for measuring the height of the Nile's waters; there are two hundred along the river

Qoz — sand-dunes

Ramadan — the Muslim month of fasting

Rotl — a measure of weight approximately equal to a pound

Sabaloga Gorge — the Sixth Cataract, 65 km north of Khartoum. At this 23 m wide gorge the waters of the Blue and White Niles actually mix. The river becomes green/grey in colour from which **eau de nil** derives its name

Saoud — snuff. The Sudanese make it into a small ball and put it behind their lower lip

Saqia — a water wheel, traditionally ox drawn

Shaduf — a lever for raising water

Sharia — a Muslim law

Sheikh — a village headman

Sudd — a barrage, more particularly the vast swamp area of the Upper Nile

Sunt — a wooded area

Tariqa — a Muslim religious order

Tebeldi — the baobab tree

Tioc — the flood plain of the Nile on which the Dinka graze their cattle

Tobe — a 9 m length of material, similar to a sari, worn by Sudanese women

Wadi — a seasonal river

Part 3
Kenya

Between Lokichokio and Lodwar: This region is the home of the Turkana people. The route from Kapoeta passes through semi desert and arid territory until the Cherangani Plateau north of Kitale.

Contents: Kenya

Kenya — Basic Information

Area: 582,645 sq. km

Population: 15½ million (including: 150,000 Asians; 40,000 Europeans; 30,000 Arabs).

Geography: The north and north east of the country is semi-desert (two thirds of Kenya is arid) and received less than 400 mm of rain a year. The flat and arid south east is character-ised by thorn bushes and rolling savannah grasslands.

A plateau forms the south-west part of the country and supports eighty-five per cent of the population. The eastern section of the Rift Valley bisects the plateau and contains the shallow lakes of Turkana, Baringo, Bogoria, Nakuru, Naivasha, and Magadi (the world's largest source of soda ash). West of the Rift Valley the plateau gradually descends to the fertile land around lake Victoria.

White beaches, fringed with palm trees, and intermittant mangrove swamps and creeks form the 480 km coastline. A coral reef protects most of the coast.

Language: Swahili is the lingua franca; English is widely spoken.

Religion: Christianity (1½ mil Roman Catholic; 1 mil Protest-ant).

Islam: Predominantly on the Coast.

Traditional Religions — Mainly amongst older people.

Hinduism — In the Asian Community.

Government: One party Republic with a National Assembly of 158 elected members plus 12 co-opted members appointed by the President.

Head of State is President Daniel arap Moi.

Economy: The country's economy is based on the production and processing of agricultural and pastoral produce. Kenya is Africa's largest producer of tea and coffee (which accounts for over fifty per cent of Kenya's foreign exchange). The tourist industry is the largest in Africa and the country's second greatest source of foreign revenue.

Income (per capita): $220(1976)

Time: GMT + 3 hours.

Electricity: 240 volts 50 cycles.

1 The Country

Natural beauty, a pleasant climate and Western comforts — if you want them — are the ingredients of Kenya's booming tourist industry. Tourists come specifically to see wildlife in the game parks and relax on the palm fringed beaches of the coast.

What is particularly striking about the country is the variety of landscape within a comparitively small area.

Climate: The long rains are from April to June, the short rains from October to November. The hottest months are February and March, the coolest June and July. The best time to visit Kenya is between December and April, during the dry, sunny season.

Although Kenya is an equatorial country its climate is varied — mainly due to its altitude. The arid regions are hot and dry. The plateau and highlands have a temperate climate: the average temperature in Nairobi is 19°C in March and 16°C in July. The climate of the coast is tropical and hot: the average temperature in Mombasa is 27°C in March and 24°C in July. The high level of humidity is relieved by sea breezes.

HISTORY

Kenya's pre-Arab history is a record of different ethnic groups migrating around the interior.

2nd century AD	Arab traders base themselves along the coast. Their towns develop at a faster rate and independently of the interior. The mixture of Bantu (African from the interior) the Arab result in the Swahili culture and language.
1498	Vasco da Gamma arrives at Malindi. Portuguese establish themselves along the East African coast, so as to protect their trade passages with the Far East.
1700	Portuguese overthrown; Islam regains influence along the coast and continues to trade with the interior.
1820s	Arab coastal domination declines due to antislave trade movements.
1895	Britain takes a major interest in the Kenyan interior with the building of the railway to link rich Uganda to the coast (915km Mombasa to Kisumu, Lake Victoria; completed in 1901). 36,000 Indian labourers were

brought over from the Sub-Continent to build the railway. On completion 20% only stayed in Kenya: they and Indian merchants along the coast are the first generation of what is now a large Asian community in Kenya.

British East African Protectorate is established.

Early 20th century
The Colonial Government encourages Europeans to settle in and develop Kenya.

The 'White Highlands' (43,250 sq km) was allotted exclusively to the whites. The Africans of this area had to either work for the Europeans or move to the established 'Native Reserves'.

The Colonial Office suggests donating part of the Highlands for a Zionist state.

Europeans develop agriculture and industry and thus the economy. Their wealth and power also increases. The European population reaches 10,000 and Asian 23,000 by 1922.

1920s
Resentment of the Europeans leads to the forming of Kikuyu Association national movement, headed by Harry Thuku.

1946
Formation of the Kenya African Union (KAU) nationalist movement, headed by Jomo Kenyatta. The organization is predominantly Kikuyu — Kenya's largest and most influential tribal group. They had also suffered most in the 'White Highlands'.

1952-56
The Kikuyu Mau Mau revolt. The government forces eventually contain the uprising, but approximately 11,500 Kikuyu were killed; 95 Europeans and Asians and 1900 Africans (loyal to the government) lost their lives.

Africans are gradually granted greater rights.

1960
Kenyatta is released, having been imprisoned during the Mau Mau, and becomes leader of the recently formed Kenya African National Union (KANU).

1963
In May KANU wins the general election. On December 12th Kenya gains Independence and remains within the Commonwealth.

1964
Kenya becomes a Republic.   Since Independence Kenya's politics have been marked by inter tribal friction, resulting for example, in the assassination of

prominant figures like Tom Mboya (1969) and Kariuki (1975).

1978   President Jomo Kenyatta dies on 22nd August.

            Daniel Arap Moi becomes president.

On Independence non African residents in Kenya were given the option of staying on, providing they adopted Kenyan citizenship.

Over half the British farmers and just under half the Asian community (many of those who left went to Britain) remained. Certain land reforms benefitting the Africans were enforced, but generally the main private land owners continued to be European and the traders Asians.

When he became president Kenyatta's slogan was 'Harambee', meaning 'Unite'. Kenya's different ethnic groups were comparatively united and Kenya gained the reputation as the most stable country in Black Africa: An African country where the move to independence had been successful.

The transition of presidency to Arap Moi after Kenyatta's death was surprisingly smooth; this again enforced the notion of Kenya's stability.

However in recent years certain internal problems may indirectly threaten this stability: a high birth rate (3.6% a year, 1975), land shortage, unemployment, poor coffee crops, high cost of petrol and the general recession.

Visas: Visitors from Commonwealth countries (except Australia) do not require visas. Britons of Asian origin should obtain a visa. The Kenyan High Commission in London is at 45 Portland Place, London W1; tel: 01 636-2371.

Health: No vaccinations are required for entry into Kenya. Take anti-malaria tablets: the disease is rare in Nairobi and the highlands but prevalent in the hot and humid areas — particularly on the coast. Avoid swimming in lakes and slow-flowing rivers in the low parts of the country, as they may be infected with bilharzia parasites. Tap water is safe to drink unless otherwise stated. Wash all uncooked fruit and vegetables.

Business hours: Monday to Friday 8.30 am to 12.30 pm and 2 pm to 4 pm, Saturday 8.30 am to 12 noon.

Public holidays: 1st January, Easter, 1st May, 1st June (Madaraka Day — anniversary of self government), 20th October (Kenyatta Day), 12th December (Independence Day), 25th December. The Eid Fitr and Eid El Adha are also celebrated.

Money: Foreign currency brought into Kenya must be declared on a currency - declaration form on entry. Exchange transactions should be documented on the form. Kenyan currency cannot be taken out of the country.

The Kenyan currency is shillings (Ksh);   there are one hundred cents to one shilling. Coins in denominations of 5, 10 and 50 cents and 1 Ksh are in circulation, and   notes in denominations of 5, 10, 20, 100 Ksh. The exchange rate is 18 Ksh to £1 sterling, 7.5 Ksh to $US1.

Banking hours are Monday to Friday 9 am to 2 pm, Saturday 9 am to 11 am.

Embassies in Nairobi:
American: Cotts House, Wabera Street, PO Box 30137.
British: Bruce House, Standard Street, PO Box 30465;
Egyptian: Total House, Koinage Street, PO Box 30285;
Sudanese: Shankdass House, Government Road, PO Box 48784;

Personal Safety
It is unwise to walk alone after dark in Nairobi, Mombasa and the resorts along the coast.

2   The Route to Nairobi

For the traveller who has made the journey from Egypt via
Sudan to Kenya, it is obvious how much a through railway
would benefit the three countries.

In Egypt, despite rumours of a southward extension to the
Sudan frontier at Wadi Halfa, nothing has been done.
The Sudanese infrastructure is particularly poor; there are no
railways or asphalt roads linking Sudan with its neighbours.
Kenya is also fairly isolated — but for a different reason. The
country's communications are relatively good, but border
problems with its neighbours have meant that surface traffic to
and from Kenya is restricted.

Ironically, the only border open without restrictions (at the time
of writing) is that with the Sudan where the road is no more than
a seasonal track at present, although future developments are
planned.

Its about 50 km from the vaguely defined border between Sudan
and Kenya to Lokichokio. The road, unsurfaced and in poor
condition, passes through barren, semi-arid desert with small
hilly outcrops.

Lokichokio is the first settlement you reach in Kenya along
this route. The sand swept army base comprises a few barrack
huts and tents; there are no shops. As this is the frontier post,
your passport and luggage will be checked, and you will
probably have to fill in a currency declaration form. If they do
not give you an entry stamp here, ask the official where you
should go to get one.

The road continues for a distance of about 230 km south east
to **Lodwar**. The surrounding landscape slowly turns to stony
desert. This area is the home of the Turkana people.

Lodwar consists of a main street with shops, a couple of cafés,
army barracks, a petrol pump and several Kenyan-styled hotels.
These hotels usually comprise a row of one-bedded breeze-block
cubicles with communal washing facilities. The charge is about
25 Ksh. per night.

People passing through Lodwar (lorry drivers travelling to or
from Sudan invariably spend a night here) treat it as an 'oasis'
in the middle of this harsh wilderness. It has a cowboy-town
atmosphere: Kenyan White Cap and Tusker beers flow freely in
the town's two bars; Turkana tribesmen squat outside the
general store and sell their handicrafts.

It's possible to find vehicles going east to Lake Turkana
(about 35 km).

Collecting water from the river, Lodwar: Lodwar is the first town in Kenya along this route. For those travelling from the south of Sudan the most significant commodities available here are petrol and cheap beer. It is possible to find transport from Lodwar to Lake Turkana.

Lake Turkana, formerly Lake Rudolph because Count Teleki of Austria (who discovered the lake in 1888) named it after his crown prince Rudolph, is the world's largest alkaline lake. The area around the serene and mystic Lake Turkana (sometimes called the Jade Sea and the largest of the string of lakes in the Rift Valley) has been referred to as the Cradle of Mankind: it was here that anthropologist Richard Leakey discovered evidence of man's earliest existence. The shores of the lake have a variety of wildlife — including crocodiles, and fishing is the main occupation of the local tribes; Nile perch of up to 100 Kg. are regularly caught.

On the west side of the lake there is accommodation at the Lake Turkana Angling Club and at Eliye Springs (40 Ksh per night for a hut). However, most travellers camp on the shores. If you chose to do this bring some food. Dingies can be hired at Eliye Springs for fishing, but be careful of the dangerous squalls that suddenly blow down the lake.

It's about an eight-hour drive from Lodwar south to Kitale. The terrain remains flat, stony and desolate until you start the ascent of the Cherangani Plateau. European contractors are building an asphalt road from Kitale via Lodwar and Kapoeta to Juba. On completion (in the mid 1980's) the road will facilitate the transport of goods from Mombasa to Juba. Because of the problems of Sudan's infrastructure, south Sudan will probably increase its imports via Mombasa in preference to Pt Sudan.

Kitale, pleasantly situated in a rich wheat, coffee and sisal growing area, was founded in 1920 by European farmers; it is still the home of a number of British expatriates. Shops are well stocked and food is readily available. From here to Nairobi (380 km) the journey is more comfortable. Between the 'matatu' park (a matatu is the Kenyan equivalent of the Sudanese box) and the lorry park there are a couple of cheap hotels. The Youth Hostel is 10 km out of town on the Eldoret road. Kitale is the best base for trips around the Mt. Elgon national park — approximately 30 km to the west (see Game Parks).

A bus (and lorries) leaves daily from Kitale to Nairobi. The journey takes about eight hours and costs 50 Ksh.

Most of the route passes along the floor of the Rift Valley. The scenery is often spectacular. After travelling through Sudan what is most striking about Kenya (besides its obvious Western influence) is its greenery and comparatively short distance between settlements. **Eldoret,** is 70 km south-east of Kitale. There is an overnight train from Eldoret to Nairobi (first class 130 Ksh., second class 60 Ksh.).

A further 155 km south-east is **Nakuru,** Kenya's farming capital (particularly well known for its pyreathrum) and third largest city; it is also the centre of what used to be the 'White Highlands', farming reserve which until twenty years ago was owned exclusively by Europeans. 8 km to its south is Lake Nakuru National Park (See Game Parks).

Continuing along the Rift Valley for approximately 70 km you come to **Lake Naivasha,** which has a large bird sanctuary and is popular with fishing enthusiasts (accommodation and camping facilities are available here). It's a further 45 km before you ascend the Kikuyu Escarpment of the Rift Valley and make the final 40 km of the journey to **Nairobi.**

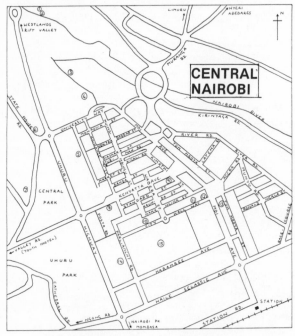

Central Nairobi		8	Post Office
1	National Museum	9	New Stanley Hotel
2	Snake Park	10	City Hall
3	Norfolk Hotel	11	Hilton Hotel
4	University of Nairobi	12	Tourist Office
5	Airways Terminal	13	Ambassadeur Hotel
6	YMCA	14	Parliament
7	YMCA	15	City Square

3 Nairobi

Nairobi (Popn.:- 776,000, 1977) — founded as a railway headquarters by the Europeans at the end of the last century — is Kenya's Westernized capital. It has little to offer the tourist in the way of sights. The two main places of interest are the Nairobi National Park (see Game Parks) and the National Museum (on Museum Road off the Uhuru Highway to the north of the town centre) which includes a collection of East African fauna and ethnographic exhibits (open daily from 9.30 am to 6 pm). Opposite the museum — and with the same opening hours — is Nairobi's snake park. Also worth a visit for those buying handicrafts is the City Market on Muindi Mbingu Street and Tubman Road. Nairobi's purpose for most tourists is as a base from where they can make excursions to the game parks, the coast and other places of natural beauty.

Where to Stay

The following details are of cheap central accommodation where you can expect to pay around 25 Ksh per person a night for a shared room: The boarding houses in and around River Road are popular with travellers. Of these the **Iqbal Hotel** in Latema Road is probably the cheapest and best known. In this area you will also find hotels of various standards charging between 50 Ksh and 150 Ksh a night.

Other popular places to stay include **Madame Roche's** (Parklands Avenue, opposite the Aga Khan Hospital), five minute ride from the town centre on bus number 11 or 12. The **Youth Hostel** (Ralph Bunche Road, off Valley Road — a continuation of Kenyatta Avenue on the other side of the Uhuru Highway) is about fifteen minutes walk from the town centre. The **YMCA** (State Road, off Uhuru Highway) is more expensive but offers full board.

For the following moderately priced centrally located hotels you can expect to pay an average of 200 Ksh for a single room:

Ambassadeur Hotel, Moi Avenue.
Excelsior Hotel, Kenyatta Avenue.
New Mayfair Hotel, Parklands Road.
Ngong Hills Hotel, Ngong Road.

The following top hotels charge anything from 300 Ksh for a single room:

Nairobi Hilton Hotel, off Mama Ngina Street.
New Stanley Hotel, Kimathi Street.
Norfolk Hotel (the famous colonial hotel), Harry Thuku Road.
Panafric Hotel, Kenyatta Avenue.
Serena Hotel, Nyere Road/Kenyatta Avenue.

Where to Eat

There are many cheap eating places around River Road, Tom Mboya Street and Moi Avenue: The **Supreme Hotel** (River Road) and the **Curry Pot** (Moi Avenue, near Moktar Daddah Street) both serve good curries; the **Satkar** (Moi Avenue) is recommended for its bhelpuris (mixture of Indian snacks) and the Safeer (near River Road) has a popular Kurdish menu.

The **Thorn Tree Cafe,** outside the New Stanley Hotel in Kimathi Street, is a well known-rendezvous for travellers and serves inexpensive hamburgers, chips and salad.

The following restaurants are moderately priced, central and popular: **Sunflower/Moonflower** (Bruce House, off Standard Street) and the **Red Bull Cafe** (Kenyatta Avenue) serve mixed grills, sandwiches and salads; the **Hong Kong,** Chinese (Koinange Street); **Arturo,** Italian (next to the Kenya cinema in Moi Avenue); the **Steak House** (Kaunda Street, near Kimathi Street); the **Ambassadeur Hotel,** general menu (Moi Avenue); the **African Heritage** (Kenyatta Avenue) recommended for its 'eat-as-much-as-you-like' African buffet — annexed to it is one of Nairobi's better handicraft shops.

Of the more expensive restaurants the following are recommended: The Tamarind, Bima House; Marinos, Italian cuisine in International House, Mama Ngina Street; The Akasaka, Japanese restaurant in the 680 Hotel in Standard Street. In addition, as one would expect, the top hotels have expensive and usually good restaurants.

Useful Addresses

Tourist Office: Corner of Moi Avenue and City Hall Way.
Post Office: Kenyatta Avenue, near Uhuru Highway.
Railway Station: Southern end of Moi Avenue, beyond Haile Selassie Avenue.

4 Game and National Parks

Wildlife abounds in Kenya. Lion, leopard, elephant, rhino, buffalo, giraffe,cheetah and plains game are just some of the animals which roam the parks mentioned below. Many tour operators organize trips to the parks, but their prices are generally high (Kimbla Ltd. off Market Street, Nairobi are a reasonably priced organization who specialize in camping safaris for low budget travellers). The only realistic alternative (in most cases there is no public transport to the parks) is to rent a car with a few friends. If you are in search of a companion, put a notice on the board at the Thorn Tree Cafe or the Youth Hostel. Most parks have well equipped lodges; however, many visitors hire tents, take their own food and camp. There is usually an admission charge; for details of this and accommodation consult the Tourist Office in Nairobi.

Main Parks North of Nairobi

Marsabit National Park (595 km north of Nairobi and 260 km north of Isiolo) covers an area of 595 sq km within the 2000 sq km of the Marsabit Game Reserve. It is a region of arid wilderness, except for the forested area around the 1700 m high Mt. Marsabit. The park is particularly well known for its long tusked elephants. This is the home of the Rendille, Boran and Gabre, who are camel riding nomads of this region. The park is open throughout the year, though the dry season is the best time for a visit.

Samburu-Isiolo Game Reserve (350 km north of Nairobi and 53 km east of Isiolo) is 300 sq km. It has a large variety of animals including the reticulated giraffe and the gerenuk, which are fairly uncommon elsewhere in Kenya. The park is divided into the thornscrub Samburu Reserve to the north of the Uaso Nyiro River and to the south the savannah grass of the Isiolo Buffalo Springs Game Reserve. The park is open all the year, however, the best time to visit is the dry season.

Meru National Park (355 km north-east of Nairobi and 35 km east of Meru) is a fairly isolated park (820 sq km) rich in game. The northern part is open savannah with swampy patches, while the south is characterized by thornbush. The park is famous as the only habitat in Kenya of the white rhino. The white rhino does not really differ from the normal rhino in colour, but in certain features and size; it is bigger, weighing up to 5 tons, and is the second largest land mammal in the world after the elephant. Meru was the home of Elsa, the lioness from the book and film 'Born Free'. The park is open throughout the year though once again the dry season is the best time to visit.

Mount Kenya National Park (200 km north of Nairobi) is one of Kenya's greatest attractions because of the spectacular views from the hiking routes around the mountain. Mt Kenya is the second highest mountain in Africa after Kilimanjaro (19,340ft/5,894m). Its four highest peaks are Batian (17,058 ft/5,199m), Nelion (17,022 ft/5,188m), Point Lenana — formerly Point Piggott — (16,625 ft/4,957m) and Point John (16,020 ft/4,882m). Point Lenana, sometimes known as 'The Tourist Mountain' can easily be climbed by fit walkers. The higher peaks are rather more difficult.

The Town of Nanyuki and the Naro Moro Camp on the west side of the mountain are good bases for trekkers. There are huts along the hiking routes where you can stay. Full information on the mountain is available from Naro Moro. The best time to visit Mt Kenya is from mid January to mid February and from September to October; avoid trekking during the rains.

Mount Elgon National Park (400 km north west of Nairobi and and 30 km west of Kitale) is the seventh highest mountain in Africa (Wagagei Peak is 4725 m) straddles the Kenyan-Ugandan border. The park covers an area of 120 sq km; its main attractions are the mountain walks along defined paths to the Elgon summit.

Nakuru National Park (155 km north-west of Nairobi and 8 km south of Nakuru) includes the Lake Nakuru, which is the world's largest reserve of flamingoes (mainly of the lesser type) and one of the finest bird lakes anywhere with over four hundred species. The lesser flamingoes feed on algae which has carotene pigment; this results in the pink colour of the birds' feathers. December and January and May and June are the best times to see the flamingoes.

Abedere National Park (160 km north-west of Nairobi and 10 km west of Nyeri; access is also possible from Naivasha some 15 km to the south in the Rift Valley) covers 770 sq km which include the Abedere mountains. The woodland and moorland park is particularly popular for walks. The famous Tree Tops hotel is situated in Abedere and it is from here that wildlife — in particular rhino, elephant and buffalo — are best viewed. The park is open throughout the year.

Main Parks South of Nairobi

Masai Mara (250 km west of Nairobi and 80 km south west of Narok) is an extension of the Tanzanian Serengeti National Park. This park, with its beautiful grassland plains and acacia woodlands abounding with wildlife, covers 1800 sq km and is one of the most popular places in Kenya to see game. The annual mass migration of zebra and wilderbeeste which passes through here is particularly fascinating. Except for rare occasions during the rainy season the park is open throughout the year; the dry season is the best time to visit.

Nairobi National Park (5 km south of Nairobi) is a convenient place to see game for those unable to make it to the larger game parks. There is also an animal orphanage at the main entrance. The park covers 120 sq km and is open throughout the year.

Amboseli National Park (180 km south-east of Nairobi) covers 3200 sq km of mainly dry savannah and areas of acacia forest. The great attraction here is Mt. Kilimanjaro (5894 m), Africa's highest mountain. Most of the mountain is in Tanzania, thus ascent from the Kenyan side of the border is not possible. The park is plentiful in game, with giraffe being particularly well represented. The park is open throughout the year, though the best time to visit is between December and February.

Tsavo National Park (250 km south-west of Nairobi, on the Nairobi-Mombasa road) is the biggest game park in East Africa covering 20700 sq km — a land area greater than Wales. The park is flat semi-arid savannah with acacia woods. This is the home of the largest elephant population in the world; however severe droughts in the 1960s and '70s — in addition to poaching — have reduced their numbers dramatically. Lion, rhino, giraffe and plains game also roam the park. Tsavo is open all the year round, though game is most bountiful between January and March.

5 The Coast

The white sanded, palm fringed beaches give Kenya one of the most beautiful coastlines in the world. This, in addition to sun, a warm pleasant climate and clear blue sea (bathers are protected from sharks by a coral reef), has led the Kenyan government to exploit the 480 km coast for tourism. An increasing number of expensive hotels along the beaches now cater for European package tours. Cheaper accommodation, including camp sites, can also be found at most towns and beaches.

Mombasa (478 km south-east of Nairobi) on an island, is Kenya's chief port and second largest city with a population of 371,000, 1977. Originally an Arab and Persian settlement from the 11th century, it became a Portuguese port of call for ships going to India after Vasco da Gama dropped anchor here in 1498. The following centuries saw Arabs and Portuguese fighting for a dominant position in Mombasa. By the end of the 17th century the Sultan of Muscat and Oman had conquered much of the East African coast. In the early 19th century the sultanate moved from Muscat and based itself in Zanzibar and it was up until Kenya's independence in 1963 that Zanzibar's flag flew in Mombasa. Today the port — cosmopolitan with Arabs, Africans, Europeans and Asians — retains much of its Arab character. Unlike the rest of the coast, Mombasa has as oppressive, humid climate. The popular Nyali beach is 3 km north of the city.

In recent years it has been disturbing to note the increased rate of muggings along the coast. However, in an endeavour to put an end to such crime the police now station watchmen on the main beaches.

It would be futile to try and mention all the resorts along the coast as each year sees new developments for holidaymakers. Below is a list of the most popular and well known coastal places. All are accessible by public transport from Mombasa.

To the south of Mombasa (distances are from Mombasa):
Tiwi Beach (21 km).
Diani Beach (37 km).

To the north of Mombasa:

Shanzu Beach (13 km).

Mtwapa Creek (18 km).

Kilifi Creek (57 km); it is necessary to catch a ferry to cross the creek.

Gedi (105 km) is the ruins of a 13th century Arab city. The remains now include a palace, mosques and a number of houses.

Watamu Beach (105 km) and Watamu Marine Park where it is possible to snorkel amongst the beautiful coral reefs.

Malindi (122 km), an old Portuguese settlement, is Kenya's most popular beach resort. Here there is also a spectacular marine park off Casuarina Point; snorkelling amongst the coral reefs is possible.

Robinson Island (approximately 160 km) is well known for its excellent fish restaurant.

Lamu (347 km), situated on Lamu island, is a delightful Arab town dating from the 14th century. Despite being a very popular tourist attraction — in particular with travellers — Lamu has not given way to development and still retains its strong Arab character, narrow streets and white coral houses. There are some fine beaches in the vicinity. Arab dhows often take passengers from Lamu to Mombasa.

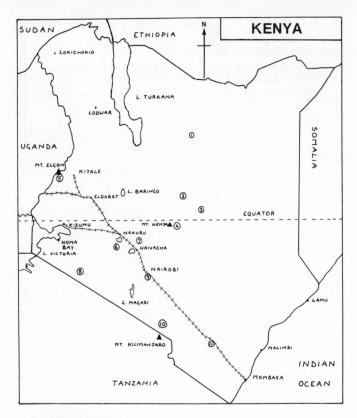

1   Marsabit Nat. Park
2   Samburu - Isiolo Game Res.
3   Meru Nat. Park
4   Mt. Kenya Nat. Park
5   Mt. Elgon Nat. Park
6   L. Nakuru Nat. Park
7   Abedere Nat. Park
8   Masai Mara Game Res.
9   Nairobi Nat. Park
10 Amboseli Nat. Park
11 Tsavo Nat. Park

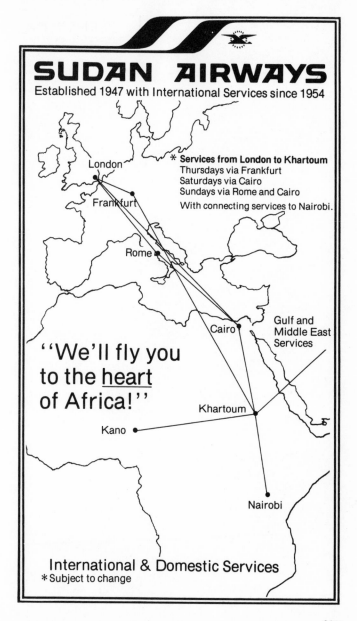

SUDAN AIRWAYS

Established 1947 with International Services since 1954

* Services from London to Khartoum
Thursdays via Frankfurt
Saturdays via Cairo
Sundays via Rome and Cairo

With connecting services to Nairobi.

London

Frankfurt

Rome

Cairo

Gulf and
Middle East
Services

Khartoum

Kano

''We'll fly you
to the <u>heart</u>
of Africa!''

Nairobi

International & Domestic Services
* Subject to change

231